RAISED AS A LIE

RAISED
AS A LIE

DR. NAEEMA K. OLATUNJI

NEW DEGREE PRESS

RAISED AS A LIE

ISBN   978-1-63730-811-0   *Paperback*
        978-1-63730-873-8   *Kindle Ebook*
        978-1-63730-977-3   *Ebook*

Kamau, Sahkiya, and Kinan

My three hearts outside of my body

CONTENTS

"You're ugly!" she yelled. "Your skin is dirty!" "Your hair is dirty!"

The only defense I have comes out in just above a whisper.

"It is not, I took a bath last night."

I cast my eyes down at my lap, tried to hide the pain. Sadly, the game I had been playing was over. My imagination was my only retreat. It was the only place where I could be a hero and not the despised villain.

Ignoring my words, Michelle raised her voice even louder to drown out my protests:

"Your skin is stained dirty. You're NEVER gonna get it clean!"

My eyes burned; my vision clouded over from the tears welling up in my eyes. I will them to stay in place.

"Why are you still here? Nobody wants you. Jim don't want you. Mommy don't want you. She just felt sorry for you, she adopted you. Just picked you up from the corner. That's why you don't look like anyone of us!"

I lose the battle, and the pain overwhelms my defenses. The anguish surrenders my shoulders. Tears pour from the corners of my eyes. Hunched over in defeat, my words sound more like a plea than a certainty.

"Mommy does want me." My doubt was causing even more pain.

"No, she doesn't! Nobody does. We are all gonna leave one night when you're asleep. We'll be gone when you wake up. You'll see."

Her torments only ever ceased after I am reduced to sobs. My suffering seemed to trigger some internal satisfaction for her. Pleased with herself, Michelle climbs down, leaving me to once again beg God to make me look like my family.

INTRODUCTION

A devastating global pandemic paralyzed our world in 2020. Simultaneously, the brutal murder of George Floyd triggered systemic racism to take center stage once again. One more Black man murdered, adding to the long list of lives taken at the hands of police. Safety felt nonexistent, and calling 911 while Black felt dangerous. Those of us mothers with teenage Black boys feared for our sons. Pleading with them every time they left the house.

"If you get pulled over, please dear God keep your hands where they can be seen! Please don't say anything that might be construed as argumentative! Most importantly, call me immediately and keep me on speaker phone!"

White America, finally awakened from their numb state of denial, could no longer legitimize police brutality. Its lethal impact provoked nationwide civil unrest followed by demonstrations, protests, and riots. The world was watching and America was the epicenter for a racial reckoning.

COVID-19 and Black Lives Matter became household words. Fear fueled our daily lives. Impossible to ignore, and heartbreaking to endure. For some, it distilled clarity that health is our one true asset. Mandated to stay at home, international lockdowns compelled us all to examine our lives and question our life choices. Business as usual was no longer an option.

So many questions and very little certainty. Life is precious. Life is short. Those two truths were irrefutable. I watched many brave souls reinvent themselves, choosing to live with purpose even if that meant huge career pivots and venturing into the unknown.

For me, 2020 brought an incredible romantic love. Divorced for nearly six years, I had begun fearing growing old alone, a veritable cat lady. Only I hate cats. In the midst of grieving a tragic unexpected family death, I fell in love with the man of my dreams, my forever man, or so I believed. I was euphoric, invincible, and freer than I had ever felt. Life is fleeting. Gyasi's death taught me that. Tomorrow is not promised. I decided to do something terrifying amid this vulnerability. I chose to say yes to becoming an author; an unspoken secret dream of mine for years. A tale I had never fully told to anyone; I said yes to telling my story of growing up as a lie.

Ironically, the love story that inspired me to say yes to writing a book, ended in devastating heartbreak. My forever love was inexplicably ending and its abruptness rocked me to my core. The moment he walked out, I felt out of control. Violently, I shook my head from side to side repeatedly until it spun. I was desperate to deny the reality. I had been on my knees begging when he pushed past me to the door. Kneeling on the floor in the wake of his departure, my hands aching from gripping his pants, I was drowning in equal parts of tears and snot. I knew I had lost who I was. To know me is to know I am ambitious, headstrong, and used to being in control. To know me is to know that I do not beg, for anything. How had I fallen that far?

Looking back, I can see those moments were necessary. The truth was, I had fallen in desperate love with someone who could never have given me what I sought. Now I had to answer why. Why was I so afraid to ask for what I needed? Here I was, a capable forty-nine-year-old mother of three, entrepreneur, doctor, business owner, podcast creator, and host. And yet there I was, begging on my knees, clutching onto a man's jeans like he was my lifeline, like he was the last helicopter out of Saigon. That excruciating pain required a deep exploration into what made me, me. My pain is why I wrote this book.

What I hadn't realized is that I had positioned this man not only in the center of my heart, but also as the center of my life. When he walked out, I attached the meaning that I couldn't live without him. That there was something wrong with me. That I wasn't worth staying and fighting for. Therapy taught me that's called a fear of abandonment. The glaring questions that followed were: Who told me I was not worthy of unconditional love? How many adult decisions in my life had come as a result of me being afraid to ask for what I needed?

Therapy also showed me that I had spent the majority of my life forgetting. Forgetting the hurtful words, forgetting the deceit, forgetting the lies, forgetting the abandonment. So much forgetting that I am actually missing years of my history because at some unknown point, the forgetting took on a life of its own. Hence, if winning an argument requires my memory, I'm forfeiting.

In 2021, I turn fifty. This birthday feels so pivotal to me. It seems as if I have waited my entire life to fully find peace in my own skin. To exhale and believe mine is an important story to tell. This is a story of a young brown girl (me) who felt invisible her entire life. Then, the only life she knew imploded when at nearly eighteen, her mother's lie is revealed. Tormented by her older sister, haunted by her obvious physical differences and a family's denial, she embarked on a journey searching for her identity. She is now tasked with reconciling her past while embracing her heritage.

Most people know who their parents are. I thought I did for a long time. Until the day I didn't. Family gives you identity. It arranges you in the microcosm of society. Yet my life proves that wrong. I didn't fit, anywhere. What happens when the most concrete aspect of your identity is that you don't have one? In my experience, you become invisible. My forty-nine-year-old meltdown proved to me that childhood traumas are not temporary and do not stay in childhood. Subconsciously, those traumas infiltrate every adult decision made, large and small. This book is my self-exploration process and that journey has led me to figure out who I am in the world.

This book is for the woman who looks back over her life, with her accoutrements of success and accomplishments and still questions her worthiness. My hope, in these pages, is that she finds the courage to heal the parts of her life that hurt. That by sharing my narrative, I am a vessel of healing. One of the most valuable lessons I learned is that there's strength in vulnerability.

In this book, you'll journey beside me as I move from brokenness, to tenacity, and ultimately, to healing.

CHAPTER 1

Randlett was a rural farming community in the early 1970s, with most of the families needing their children to help work the land. We were hay farmers. Everyone on a farm works. The chores start at near dawn, and depending on the season, work lasts until sundown. The county's board of education became concerned that the farming children weren't prepared to enter first grade because they lacked the capacity to sit still in school desks for hours at a time. I agreed. The last thing I wanted to do every day was to sit in a hard wooden straight-back chair for what felt like an eternity. Despite my objections, when I was four-and-a-half, my mother enrolled me in the town's Headstart program. No one asked my opinion and I didn't get a vote.

"It's only a few hours in the mornings," she had said, trying her best to put a nice spin on it. "You'll make friends."

"Jughead is my friend," I said, referring to my beloved horse. But my protests fell on deaf ears. I knew her mind was already made up.

My entire morning routine was all about to be ruined because of school. First came feeding the chickens, then the pigs, then circling back to collect the chicken eggs from the hen coop, and finally ending with a visit with my favorite animal on the farm. Jughead, an eighteen-year-old, brown spotted horse, was my best friend. Truth be told, he was my only friend. Besides my sister, the only kids I ever played with were Jim's two nephews. Jim was father to me and my baby brother, William. He was tall, blonde, and as short-tempered as he was quick-tongued with verbal insults. He ruled with an iron fist and drank frequently, yet never managed to be a happy drunk. His dangerous blue eyes would flash and turmoil followed like the stench from a pig pen. I always thought the nephews were odd so we didn't play very often. They were two sandy-blonde-haired boys, ages eight and nine, whose only goal in life was to watch the chickens race down the path after their heads had been chopped off. The boys would make bets on which beheaded chicken would run the farthest.

By my fifth birthday, I already knew how to catch and skin wild rabbits, wring chicken necks, pluck chickens clean, and milk cows. Once saddled on Jughead, I could also help Jim wrangle the sheep. I'd follow Jim everywhere around the farm, a veritable farmhand assistant. I loved the land and soaked up everything I learned. On summer days, I'd be hard at work, shirtless like Jim with a janitor-size key ring full of lucky rabbit's feet hanging from the belt loop on my pants.

Liza, my mom's faithful German shepherd, went everywhere with me. Since my mom had had my baby brother, she was often tired and couldn't keep a watchful eye on my activities. I swear my mom paid Liza under the table to babysit me. If Liza wasn't by my mom's side, she was attached to my hip. I never really minded though; Liza was a good listener and was always willing to play.

I tried in vain to reason my way out of going to school, but my mom was born with an extra DNA strand of stubbornness. I lost the argument to skip the whole school business. Of course, I would lose. No one, except Jim, ever actually won an argument with my mom, or Sandy, as she was nicknamed. Born Sandra Jean Panno, the eldest of six children, she grew up in Detroit, Michigan. She was fierce, demanding and bossy; yet comforting and had a huge heart, especially for the underdog. She was five-feet-six inches tall, with dark hair and fiery green eyes. Since age eleven, she had been in charge of her five younger siblings when her mother had a nervous breakdown. She had grown tough; she had to be, two of those siblings were tenacious brothers. It was her job to raise and protect them in a city known for its three C's: crime, corruption, and cars.

My grandfather (her father) would often say: "Your mother could out-stubborn a mule."

I don't know if I will ever fully understand my mother; she was complex and hurt and dealt with her own baggage, just as we all do. Some of her decisions will never make sense to me, but my love and admiration for her are no less. I never walked in her shoes, but I know she loved her kids with all of her heart and did the best she could do.

She yelled a lot, but the only curse words she ever used were "damn" and "pissed off." She took pride in everything she did. She loved her family. She was a loyal friend. She wasn't late to a thing in her life, and she'd accuse me of being late to my own funeral. She was honest and she hated liars, which is so weird to say since she lied to me my whole life. Maybe that's why she demanded honesty in all other parts of her life.

My mother didn't seem to ever miss a thing; it seemed she had two sets of eyes behind her head. I think she had been mothering for so long that she simply didn't know how not to. She always had a hug and a kiss to give our bumps and bruises with a Band-Aid never far behind. She'd also swat your fanny the moment you got out of line, and she wasn't opposed to finding the belt for greater offenses.

On my first day of school, I was up early to get my chores done. Jim was on another one of his drinking benders and had been gone for several days. When he was absent, my mom was burdened with all the farming chores and still had us kids and the house to tend to. I wanted to at least do my part and still have time to wash up. The oldest of us kids was my sister Michelle, my senior by seven years. Eleven years old, blonde hair, blue eyes, and a tad on the chubby side. I idolized my sister. She was incredibly smart and an extremely talented artist. She could draw almost anything she imagined. Michelle, however, was in a perpetual state of anger. As such, she was rarely ever nice to me. She gave great performances in front of the adults as the older protective sister. The reality, however, was the only person Michelle ever protected was Michelle.

Her routine was to call me names and tell me I was dirty, unwanted, and unloved. Her ammunition? I didn't look like anyone in our family. Her name-calling and venom would surface, and I'd become her target. I didn't have the vocabulary or the communication skills to discredit her accusations. She was masterfully sneaky and devious, always making sure adults were out of earshot. No one was ever the wiser of her terror targeted only at me.

Michelle's words were even more painful because I knew she was right. Not one person had my brown skin or wild curly hair. They all had light eyes, mine were dark. Even four-year-olds have enough life experience to understand identity and I was the one who didn't fit.

I doubted my mom's optimism of going to school and making new friends. I had no reason to believe that they would like me. Hadn't Michelle made that clear? Hadn't she told me countless times that no one would ever like me? On that morning, I was so nervous and desperate to prove Michelle wrong. My morning prayer was to make just one friend.

"Your skin is dirty," echoed in my head as I washed up. Scared the other kids would think the same, I scrubbed my skin nearly raw.

When it was time, my mom, carrying my three-month-old brother, walked me the two acres to the main road to await the bus's arrival. Turned out it wasn't the kids I had to be wary of after all; it was the teacher.

I walked into my new classroom and the sounds of fifteen four-year-olds running and squealing greeted me. The room was brightly lit, the fluorescent lights gave the new yellow paint a strange tinge. Each of the four low round tables had four small straight-backed wooden chairs neatly arranged around them. The teacher, Ms. Wyatt, called for our attention.

"Good morning, everyone!" Ms. Wyatt cheerily announced. The class began to grow silent.

"Welcome to your new class. I will call each of your names. Then I will assign you to your new seat. Please listen carefully."

I had been eyeing another little girl with beautiful, long, jet-black hair that I hoped to sit next to. Her sleek dark tresses mesmerized me, reminding me of my mother's similar locks. She was different from all the other blonde girls. I crossed my fingers behind my back, hopeful she'd like that I was different too.

Ms. Wyatt began to call names and one by one the children took their assigned seats. The longhaired girl had just taken her seat. I was so busy staring at her hair, I didn't realize the teacher had walked right up to me.

"Excuse me. I've called your name several times and you haven't answered."

"Oh...I, uh didn't hear you," I stammered.

"You have to listen when you're being spoken to," she said sternly. "There are rules here and you must follow them. Do you understand, Barbara Lynn?"

"Um, I uh... what did you say?" Now I was just confused.

The teacher rolled her eyes at me, clearly frustrated. It had only been five minutes in her class and I'd already exhausted her patience with me. She took a deep breath and said, "Barbara Lynn, I said there are rules here and you must—"

"But I don't understand—" I interrupted, but she didn't wait for me to finish.

"You farm kids are all the same," she muttered loud enough for me to hear. "Do I need to call your mother, Barbara Lynn?"

"That is not my name!" I stood defiantly. I knew she was mad, and I didn't want her calling my mom but—

Interrupting my thoughts, the teacher sternly said, "That is your name and we are calling your mother!"

"Fine!" My hands were crossed over my chest now. "It's Grace."

"What's grace?"

"My name. It's Grace."

"It absolutely is not!" Ms. Wyatt's face looked like she had just eaten something sour and her cheeks reddened. She grabbed my arm and walked us both over to the big olive-green rotary phone hanging on the wall. I listened to the one-sided conversation. Then I heard her telling my mom that she needed to come and pick me up.

"She is defiant and will not follow my rules," she said, exasperated.

I stopped listening. I jutted my chin out indignantly and pursed my lips tight over my teeth. My face felt hot and I clenched my small hands into fists at my sides. I looked up and all the kids were watching me. Reflexively, my back muscles stiffened like when riding too fast on Jughead. My heart thudded so loud in my chest I feared everyone could hear it. I knew I shouldn't have come to this dumb place with the ugly paint and a pinched-face teacher. Clearly, my mom had made a mistake; she chose a very dumb teacher who doesn't even know her students' names.

Suddenly, I heard my mother's laughter through the phone receiver Ms. Wyatt was holding. My mother's voice was deep and melodic, her laugh full, robust, and contagious. I saw the corners of Ms. Wyatt's mouth turn up reluctantly. I couldn't imagine why on earth my mother was laughing.

My mother borrowed her in-laws' car to drive into town to the school, since Jim had his truck. She walked into the class with my baby brother still in her arms. I swear she never put that kid down. My mother saw me standing in the far corner, isolated from the rest of the class, where the teacher sentenced me to stand. She walked toward me, pulled a kid-sized chair over, and sat down. I saw her trying to compose her face. *Was she trying not to laugh?* I thought for sure I'd be in trouble, but she was laughing at me. *Nothing made sense.* My bottom lip began to quiver. *She's supposed to be on my side.* I clenched my jaw tighter to stop it from trembling, making the blood throb in my temples. I knew the kids were still staring at me, ignoring the teacher's attempts to begin the lesson. *None of this was funny to me.*

"I didn't do anything wrong!" I blurted out in protest. "The teacher kept calling me the wrong name! I am not dumb. She's dumb!" It was all I could do not to yell.

Coordination. Balance. Body awareness. Agility. Dexterity. All words one would never ever use to describe me.

I knew I was clumsy. But Grace was my name. It described ME. I was Grace.

"Honey, I know. I know. It's just..." Her voice cracked and she trailed off. Her face was all screwed up, like it was taking every effort to stay composed. I searched her face for clues since I couldn't imagine how any of this was humorous. She noted my questioning look.

"Well, honey," she began again. "Your name isn't actually Grace." Her chin actually began to quiver from holding in her laughter. Again, I think, *what was so doggone funny?*

"Huh?" I reacted with absolute confusion. "It is so. That's what everyone calls me!" I challenged.

"Sweetie, it's just ... you... well ... you aren't very graceful. You fall a lot and you have lots of accidents," she nodded toward my shins.

They were covered with bruises, scrapes, and half-healed scabs, a veritable map of misguided decisions. The largest were a set of new matching purple bruises. On my morning ride with Jughead, he decided he was tired and just laid down right next to the propane tank. I was trapped in the saddle, wedged between his 1,200 pounds and the tank until my mom heard my cries. Decades later, I can still retrace my childhood from the scars on my legs and the many I have added along the way. Yes, I still say excuse me when I walk into walls.

"It was just a funny nickname that stuck, honey."

CHAPTER 2

No one who knew my mother would ever describe her as a nervous person. She was a textbook example of a type A personality. She was the most capable person I ever knew and a force to be reckoned with. This explains how a born and raised Detroit city girl adapts and flourishes in rural farm life. She never backed down to a challenge and yet her thumbs told an entirely different story.

Shortly after my fourth birthday, my mother was tending to our family garden. The strawberries were so plump and juicy my mouth watered, and my fingers ached to pick a snack. Giant, bright green broccoli stalks and heads of crisp, purple cabbage bloomed wildly and were interlaced between baby pink and blue Barge flowers. She planted sunny, bright yellow Marigold blooms just because she loved how the flowers opened up for the sun each morning. My mother hadn't met a plant or flower that wouldn't prosper for her. She had ten innate green thumbs, with an almost surreal connection with plant life. I imagine her superhero avatar would imbue the cities devastated by the villain's fiery wrath, with all new plant life as if spring was emerging.

That particular early afternoon, the cool crisp morning air had surrendered to the sun's warmth. I squatted in between the marigolds eyeing the strawberries like a fox in a hen house. My job was supposed to be to locate and remove the slugs from the strawberry foliage. However, at the moment, my hypervigilance was preoccupied with satisfying my stomach.

I loved gardening with my mom. It was the one place you'd never find my sister. Michelle's skin was so fair that any length of sun exposure would inevitably result in a blistering sunburn. The task was tedious for my four-year-old energy, but I cherished the quality alone time with Mom. I would take advantage of my captive audience and babble endlessly about my adventures on Jughead. My mom, for her part, acquiesced to listening to my ceaseless tales.

Today, however, she seemed lost in her own thoughts, distracted from pruning the petulant weeds. She kneeled, her hands caked in soil, resting in her lap. I paused mid-sentence, abandoning my berry thief plotting, to watch her fingers. I hadn't noticed the rhythmic movement pattern before. Her two index fingers seemed to move of their own accord. Slowly, yet with practiced precision, each first fingernail picked at the skin on the side of its neighboring thumb. She wasn't looking at her hands, she wasn't even looking down at the rows of lush garden leaves. Her vision cast slightly skyward but didn't appear to notice anything. Until she winced in pain.

Looking down, it was as if she saw her hands for the first time; like her arms had spontaneously sprouted them in the past two minutes. On her left hand there was a tiny pool of blood gathering at the corner of the thumb nailbed. It was then she noticed I was staring at her. Reflexively, she stiffened her back and absently swiped away the evidence across her gardening apron. When she looked up again, she offered me a weak smile.

Shyly, I kept a watchful eye on her hands the rest of the afternoon, taking note when the thumb picking would commence. My mind, young and developing, couldn't comprehend why my beautiful mother would pull her own skin off of her hands. Why would she inflict pain onto herself? I didn't know then that life-altering habits can form from brief visual encounters.

Weeks later, unbeknownst to me, I had inadvertently picked up the same habit. Unintentionally and without conscious thought, I had begun to pick the skin off the sides of my own thumbs. The outcome set me down an emotional rabbit hole that I had no language for.

Bath-time catalyzed the discovery. It was past my bedtime and I was still in the tub. My mom, usually a drill sergeant for punctuality, had relented when I pleaded for more time. My bathtub troops were still engaged in conflict. After a victorious battle between good and evil, Barbie sat on the porcelain ledge reigning over her new subjects, a trio of sunflower yellow rubber duckies. The sudsy bubbles had long since dissolved and I was getting sleepy. The last of the water drained from the tub and I stood up. Standing, the giant bath towel draped over my damp small shoulders as mom dried my legs off.

"You've been in here so long you shriveled up to a prune," she observed.

Shivering and noticing for the first time all the newly formed wrinkles on my fingers, I turned my hands over for a closer inspection. It was true, my fingers looked more like elongated raisins than they did hands. More shocking to me, were the sides of my thumbs where I had picked my own skin days earlier. It had turned white!

"Dirty knees! Dirty knees! You got dirty knees!" reverberated in my head.

"My skin is white," I whispered slowly, staring at my hands as if seeing them for the first time.

My mom, distracted, paused toweling me off and asked, "What did you say, honey?'

I stared intently at my thumbs, but the words refused to form. My thoughts were muddled. I felt disconnected from my body, almost numb. Somewhere in the distance, I heard my mom saying, "I didn't hear you, Sweetie. What did you say?"

It's as if my vocal cords were no longer taking orders from my brain. I could only see white skin.

"You're dirty! You're dirty!"

Michelle's words sounded like a shriek in my head, my ears were burning, my face was hot, my vision has tunneled into only seeing my thumbs.

My mom was shaking my shoulders, "Barbara Lynn!"

"Huh?" I heard her voice, but I could only see my thumbs...my skin was white.

Michelle's venomous words were suffocating, depriving me of oxygen. Inside, I was gasping for air, doing all that my little four-year-old self could to just breathe.

"You're dirty!"

Yet, my skin was white. Underneath, my skin was white—just like the rest of my family. My white skin was just covered up. My young, still-developing brain concluded that if I picked all the top layer of skin off my whole body, I too, would be white. Then I would look like my family. Then I would be accepted. Then I would be loved. Then I would not be dirty.

I. Would. Be. Enough.

My sister's words could no longer hurt me if I was white too. In that moment, I ceased being a child; the white skin revelation forced me to embrace emotions I had no language for. I did the only thing I could. I simply burst into uncontrollable sobs.

Even after all these years, writing this brings me to tears. I cry for that little girl. My heart aches for that little person who secretly tried to pick off all of her skin so she could have white skin like everyone else. Because she believed that once she looked like everyone else, she would know in her heart that she was loved, and she was worthy.

CHAPTER 3

"Necessity is the mother of invention" was probably coined to describe farm life. Living off the land in rural Randlett, Utah, demands full utilization of all things. Wastefulness is akin to sin on a farm, and convenience isn't expected. Life on a farm is hard work. There are no easy short cuts, and our farm was no exception.

To say there was nothing for miles in any direction from our hay farm was a vast understatement. Randlett sits in the Northeastern corner of the Uintah and the Ouray Indian reservations with three national forests hugging its borders.

In 1892, the settlement was founded and named after Colonel James Randlett, a commanding officer at Fort Duchesne Army base. It began as the site of an Indian residential school for Ute children. Also known as Native American boarding schools, these US government-funded institutions paid the Catholic and Christian churches to solve the "Indian Problem." (Broken Promises, 2018) Hundreds of these institutions were established across the country all under the banner of "kill the Indian, save the man." The battle cry was coined by Army officer Richard Henry Pratt. These so-called schools forced assimilation by Americanizing *Native American* children into *Euro-American* civility with the goal of eradicating all indigenous cultures. (Van Cott, 2021)

The strict militaristic discipline used to sever Native American children from their inherent heritage was severe and deadly. Tens of thousands of children were separated from their families and communities for extended periods of time and forced to attend these schools. Kidnapping children was a widely used tactic and white America fully accepted it as rationale that the ends justified the means. Native American fathers were imprisoned in Alcatraz for their refusal to send their children to these so-called schools. (Blad, 2020)

The schools claimed to be educating the students; however, the reality of the "education" has since been exposed through the many documented cases of abuse. Countless cases of sexual, physical, and mental abuses that occurred mostly in the church-run schools. (Maxwell, 2014) The 1928 *Meriam Report* noted that infectious disease was often widespread at these boarding schools due to malnutrition, overcrowding, poor sanitary conditions, and students weakened by manual labor overwork. The report said that death rates for Native American students were six and a half times higher than for all other ethnic groups.

In 1973, this was the town we lived in. It was nearly one hundred years after these unforgivable practices began, and Native American parents finally regained their rights to refuse attendance to these schools. The damage had been severe and thorough. The animosity between Native Americans and whites in Randlett was ever-present, like a guest who comes to dinner then becomes a permanent resident. There was a constant low-grade humming of hostility between the two races. White people in Randlett lived entitled, as if this was their land. They felt justified in the historic abusive behavior toward Native American people. The Native Americans, for their part, simply distrusted white people.

Jim's family had lived on this land for three generations. He, like his father and his father's father, hated Native Americans. Resented them, like they were the ones who had stolen the land. Jim believed Native Americans were the ones trespassing and wouldn't listen to anyone who didn't agree with him.

Late one night, all five of us were crammed into the cab of Jim's 1960 dilapidated Ford F100 truck. We were driving home from a long day fishing on the Duchesne River. Jim was driving, Michelle sat next to him, knees straddling the stick shift, then me, then my mom holding baby William on her lap. We kids were all sleeping when suddenly Jim slammed on the brakes, the tires screeched in protest and the truck lurched to the left. Baby William let out a shriek and Jim bellowed a slew of curses as he swerved the truck off the road. My mom screamed as the impact of something hard hit the truck. We finally jolted to a stop near the ditch, bordering the side of the road. My mom continued to wail. Ignoring her, Jim jumped out of the cab to inspect what he had hit. My mom covered her mouth with her hand and tried to soothe William's cries.

I twisted my body around so I could look out the back window. I could barely make out Jim walking down the two-lane road we had just driven; his dark figure only lit by the rear truck lights. There were no street lights, no houses, no porch lights to illuminate the solitary road—just pitch blackness everywhere. Suddenly, he was back behind the steering wheel with a new fury of curses.

"That goddamn Injun! Just walking on the goddamn road!" he yelled.

We were all crying now. Jim yanked down hard on the gear shift throwing the truck into overdrive. We jolted back onto the road. Terror filled my mom's eyes.

"You can't leave him! Dear God, Jim! Turn around!" screamed my mother.

Jim slammed his foot on the gas, the force fishtailing the back end of the truck. Tires screeching across the blackened asphalt was his only reply. I don't know how many miles we had gone before my mom ceased begging him to turn around. The only sound you could hear was Michelle and my soft sobs over the hum of the engine. Jim never did turn around. Never felt remorse for running a man over and most likely killing him. The man was Indian and that was all the reasoning Jim needed. As a white entitled man, Jim felt justified in leaving that poor man to die on the side of the road, dismissing him as if he was less than human. Years later, I am often jealous of baby William; he will never carry that nightmare of a memory.

————

The swing set had long since been rusted into shades of copper brown. The actual swings absent, necessity deemed that it ceased being a child's recreational toy and instead was reinvented into a slaughtered beef-hanging contraption. Although flying through the air on the swings was no longer an option, Jim added what became my favorite feature.

Technically, it was a storage area, housing the more dangerous slaughtering tools, but to me it was an open-air balcony. A bona fide treehouse sans the tree. It was made up of two sheets of bracketed plywood and attached to the top of the swing set supported by a couple of six feet two-by-fours cemented into the dirt. The makeshift tool storage created a second story of sorts. I spent hours on top of that swing set imagining sailing voyages across oceans I'd never actually seen. On this particular day, Jim was sharpening the tools in the barn, leaving me alone to create endless adventures.

Perched atop the old metal-framed swing set, I felt like I could see the whole world or at least our one hundred acres of it. On the left, was an old barn housing our pigs, cows, and horses. Jim had refused to install a proper roof, instead haphazardly constructed wood slats covered by large sheets of tarp paper served as a shelter. My mom was furious the year her brother, my Uncle Frank, visited to help harvest the hay and fell through those wood slats. We were all so relieved that he only suffered a temporarily injured back.

Adjacent to the barn, were galvanized steel pipe horse corrals and a riding arena welded from the same rusted metal. Fifty feet on the opposite side of the barn were four pig pens followed by an unpainted wood chicken coop. Most of the land around the building structures had been cleared and only dirt remained. Brush covered everything else except Mom's garden. At the northern end, near the base of Cedar Mountain and barely visible from my vantage point, was my favorite summertime spot. A large swimming pond with a homemade rope swing hanging from a nearby tree. What sat in the center of the farm was the unfinished three-bedroom ranch style house we lived in. Jim was supposed to finish the basement so it would stop flooding down there. He went on a three-day drinking binge instead. The rage he flew into after his return left Michelle with a broken wrist when she "got in the way." None of us ever brought up the basement again.

The house was three different shades of beige and yellow as we never had enough money to buy proper paint. It was a small, modest house that sat on a partially-cemented foundation. The main feature of the otherwise nondescript house was the giant sliding glass door that served as our main entryway. It was the second glass door actually. The first one met its match when one of the more curious cows, invigorated by the spring weather, walked straight through it. It took Jim a week to replace the glass and repair the giant gaping hole the invasion left.

Jim's parents owned the land and their house was off in the distant southern corner. The snowcapped peaks of Cedar Mountain were in the distance. One winter, while a foot of snow still blanketed the ground, Michelle and I followed a trail of odd-looking footprints all the way to the base of the mountain. There was one giant man's footprint and a tiny roundish imprint followed, then another giant footprint. It went on like that for the better part of a mile. Then, right as the incline to the mountain began, the prints suddenly disappeared. Rumors of Bigfoot had been circulating around the town and Michelle and I were convinced we had just seen proof.

The swing set landing had a perfect 360-degree view of the farm. I saw Michelle storm out of the barn, Jim's cruel words chasing her out. She was headed to the house, but she spotted me on the landing and made a beeline to the swing set instead. Michelle was about to ruin my impending imaginary rescue mission where I was saving a whole island of giant sea turtles who were shipwrecked and destined for certain doom.

I knew the moment she climbed up, I would bear the brunt of her fury. Michelle was powerless against Jim's abuse. She was like a sinking ship desperately trying to stay afloat. Terrorizing me was her ticket to reclaiming her power. Her ticket to set her ship back on course. Michelle couldn't control Jim's fury or the harm he inflicted upon her, but what she could control was how she treated me. How she harmed me with her poison-laced words that hurt like daggers.

Michelle attended the local school nearly fifteen miles away. Every day, she was exposed to the town's disdain toward Native Americans. Here she was, little Miss America, blonde hair and blue-eyed, born with all the physical ideals of a white- dominated country. My sister: as American as apple pie. Was her own intolerance of me reinforced by our town's demonizing anything non-white? I often wondered if her anger at my mom for moving us to this dusty, rundown farmland was fueled by being the sister to me: dark, curly-haired me, brown-skinned me.

CHAPTER 4

Before my sixth birthday, on a bright spring morning without any warning to us kids, my mother did the most unexpected thing. She made breakfast like any other morning. Michelle got on the school bus like any other day. My mom waited for Jim to leave; he was headed to the next town for feed and supplies and kissed him goodbye like any other time. Then, like a mad woman, she raced around the house grabbing what I thought were odd items and packed everything she could fit into our 1962 Ford Fairlane. Arranging everything like a Tetris puzzle, she even managed to create two beds on top in the backseat; one for me and the other for baby William, who was already eighteen months old.

I don't know how long she had been plotting her escape; what I did know is that I had never seen her so focused and simultaneously so scared. Her plan was to load the car then pick up Michelle from school during their lunchtime. She figured we'd be a third of the way on the eight-hundred-mile journey back to her parents' home in California before Jim was the wiser. Nothing, it seems, is ever that seamless.

Something in him must have caught wind of her plan because Jim unexpectedly showed up at Michelle's school at noon. All the kids were outside playing on a rare day without snow. As a precaution, my mom had parked her car down the street and we walked to the school. By the time we reached the parking lot, I knew something was very wrong. Jim was climbing back behind the wheel of his truck when he saw us. Michelle was already in the passenger seat looking scared and confused.

As soon as Jim saw my mom, he hopped down from the truck and beelined it for us. I don't know what possessed me to do it; I still wasn't clear what was happening, but I stepped in front of my mom protectively. She had baby William in her arms. Jim looked down at me, sneered and snatched my arm. As he dragged me back to his truck, all I could hear was my mom screaming. The teachers and the principal had been outside with the kids and must have heard all the commotion. They cautiously walked closer to where we were. Jim was hollering and cussing, my mom was pleading for him to let me go and William was crying.

Jim never slowed his pace. He picked me up and nearly threw me into the cab then climbed in beside me. Michelle was crying and my mom was standing on her side of the truck attempting to soothe all three of us through the window. She was trying to make peace, denying she was leaving, pleading that if he just let us go, she'd come home and they could talk it all out. Jim wasn't having any of it. He kept yelling and gesturing violently with his hands. The principal began pleading on my mom's behalf. Finally, Jim appeared to relent. He leaned over me and opened the passenger door. He barked at me to get out first. As

Michelle started to slide out, Jim grabbed the gold necklace around her neck.

The scene will forever be burned in my psyche. My terrified sister gasping for air, her eyes bulging from being strangled, the principal bellowing, kids and teachers alike screaming, and my mom beseeching God to save her child. One of the teachers had called the police. They showed up in the nick of time. Somehow one of the officers brokered a deal with Jim that he wouldn't be arrested if he'd release Michelle and go home to talk everything over with his wife.

My mother agreed but did no such thing. Once Michelle was free from Jim's capture, she urgently ushered us all into our car and took off for California. It literally looked like a movie scene, tires screeching and all. She never looked back. Occasionally, she'd look over to check on Michelle and gently touch the giant near-strangling welts on her neck. I think she drove the twelve hours without stopping. She knew that car was on its last leg. I figured the deal she had kept was with God; if she'd save her family from the abuse, he'd deliver us safely to our destination. And he did exactly that. The Fairlane died in my grandparent's driveway as soon as my mom put it into park. It never ran again.

I also believed God blessed my mom for her courage because two years later, she met Art. The man who would become my stepfather. The man who she would build a new life with. The man who would change everything, for all of us.

———

In the final summer days before my senior year, my mom and Art sold our family home in Southern California and relocated us to the second smallest town I've ever seen. Coming from the suburbs, where shades of beige stucco, cookie-cutter homes were erected every dozen feet for miles in every direction and separated by five-lane freeways, this sandy desert town was an unwelcome change. To date, I had attended five elementary schools, one middle school, and three high schools. To say we moved a lot is an understatement. I believe my mother was forever in pursuit of a better life for her family, and Art was ever in support of her quest. Each house was a bit nicer than the former. Each neighborhood displayed greater elements of wealth.

For the life of me, I couldn't figure out why she chose this little town. Maybe my mom missed the serenity of farm life in Utah. Maybe she wanted out of the suburban rat race. Either way, her decision was not popular.

I hated this new town. It was my senior year after all! I was finally supposed to be part of an envied group. I had been waiting, planning, and counting on emerging as popular (or as close to it as I'd ever been). Yet here I was, at the lowest point of my life, crying over missing my old house, my friends, my extended family, and the familiarity of my surroundings. This tiny little desert town in the middle of nowhere was so foreign to anything I'd ever known. There was sand everywhere you looked, and I hated it for everything it was not. To be fair, I think the town felt the same about me. The town boasted of its nonexistent diversity like it was a hard-earned first place ribbon at the county fair. There was one elementary school, one middle school, and one high school, and not one student in any of those classrooms was a person of color. A perfect microcosm of the town's closed mindset.

Walking onto the high school campus my first day was like entering a time warp. Living in newly constructed suburbs for the past four years, I had forgotten what old buildings smelled like. What greeted me were walls caked with layers of once brightly colored paint but now were peeling at the seams. Linoleum floors, once white turned dull yellow after years of bleaching. Faded orange and green décor that reminded me of sitcoms filmed twenty-five years ago. The front office looked like time had forgotten it; years of dust coated the hanging black and white pictures of the school's ribbon cutting thirty-five years prior. Stained shag rugs littered the floors attempting to cover up several missing tiles.

"Dear God," I whispered miserably.

After a month, my misery hadn't let up. I felt like I attended a prison each day. This was the place my happiness had been sentenced to death. For the fiftieth time in three minutes, I glanced down at my classic Mickey Mouse watch with the bright red band. It had been a sweet sixteen birthday present from my grandparents. Mercifully, it said 12:20; that's my cue to get a bathroom pass. My habit was, get out of class early, beat everyone to the cafeteria, and get my food first. Then, find a seat in the furthest corner before the rush, thereby avoiding the inevitable rejection to my "Is this seat taken?" question.

My habit was interrupted when three pasty-faced, blue-eyed, and sun-bleached blondes cornered me in the cafeteria. At first, I didn't know who these brutish-looking boys were because I was eye level to their chests. When I looked up at their faces, I recognized them as senior kids. These three were the ring leaders of the popular clique that reigned over the lunchroom like a monarchy, their subjects clamoring for their attention.

I had just walked through the main entrance when they appeared, blocking my path forward. Standing shoulder to shoulder, they looked like an offensive football line. I could hear the students pressing forward from the hall because the bell had just rung. Frustrated that the blonde trio had blockaded my plan, I glared in their direction.

All 203 high school kids from freshman to senior crowded into the stark white lunchroom. Everyone clanging the hard plastic lunch trays they were carrying against the metal rails. Sounds echoed off the bleached linoleum floors and exposed ceilings. It sounded like a two-hundred-piece toddler orchestra rehearsing, armed with metal pots and wooden spoons. Half the kids pressed each other forward forming haphazard lines. The short lunch break demanded a mad rush to reach the harried lunch ladies who, for their part, ladled out the bland, overcooked food onto a flurry of oncoming plastic plates. The crowd's momentum forced me and my bullies into the corner behind one of the large metal doors partially hiding our location.

Futilely, I attempted to keep the distance between us. The menacing looks they were launching at me signaled my fight-or-flight instincts. I'd never interacted with these boys before, but I knew instantly this wasn't friendly fire, and I was in trouble.

I could feel the hair rise on the back of my neck and chills traveled down my spine despite the heat. The ugly, ancient dial barometer above the lunch lines read 90°F. No one was paying attention to the corner I'd been pressed into. Even if I yelled, no one would hear over the racket. The boys kept inching closer hissing threats.

"Do you know what we do to people like your kind?" taunted the one closest to my right elbow.

For a moment, my panic paused. "*Your kind*" reverberating off the walls in my mind. What does he mean, *my kind?* What kind am I? The new kid kind? I mean, I've only been at the school less than a month, many of those days begging my mom to let me stay home claiming a stomach bug. The few days I've actually gone to school, I kept to myself. As if I have a choice, no one talks to me anyway.

The one on the left raised his voice to ensure I heard him over the crowd. "You hear us talking to you nigger girl?"

I almost laughed out loud despite the terror I am feeling.

Nigger girl? Is that what you think? Well, I am not Black, you moron. I think but dare not say any of this. Clearly, he ain't the smartest of the three, and I'm certain I wouldn't be the first to point that out to this band of idiots. Instead, I just stare at them.

The third boy chimed in with his best Hannibal Lecter voice:

"You know where our hangout is. We're gonna take you out there and show you what we do to nigger girls!"

The ringleader's face was flushed red, and the blue hue in his eyes blazed with hatred. "We're gonna take you out there and lynch you next to the bonfire. No one will ever hear your screams!"

I knew of their hangout spot. Everyone did. Not everyone gets invited though. I suppose it goes without saying that I had never been invited. Miles and miles of the vast, desolate desert surround the town. Somewhere deep into those sand dunes, the high school kids piled into their daddy's Chevy trucks and Duallys. They off-roaded to some undisclosed locale where you'd need advanced GPS to locate the teenage tribe.

Yes, I'd heard about their weekend jaunts. Rumors floated all over school. Although the location had yet to be public knowledge, as those invited jealously guarded the coveted secret.

Simultaneously, as if there was some silent bullying cue they had practiced dozens of times, they all stepped closer to me. Inches away from my face, I smelled their cheap colognes competing with whatever the mystery meat was on the menu. I instinctively flinched. I hated to give them the satisfaction of knowing I was afraid. In sync, they deepened their sneers. Who says white boys don't have rhythm? Knowing they had scared me bolstered their already overinflated confidence. I knew their type; intimidation was only the first chess move. Annihilation being the final. It was futile to deny it, I was afraid.

Hell, I was terrified.

I had no idea what lynching meant, but this much I was certain of: *It ain't good.*

CHAPTER 5

It felt as if time was standing still. I watched my mom incessantly wring her hands as if she was holding a water-soaked rag. We sat in silence, alone in her room. She didn't speak and I felt her anxiety, saw her fingers pick at the thumb skin. I listened to her breathing become more rapid and increasingly shallow as if the oxygen had suddenly diminished. This was *not* my mother. I hadn't seen her this shaken up since the "Jim days," the name I'd given those six, long years. Whatever she was about to say was clearly tormenting her. Down the hall, the deep baritones of the large grandfather clock echoed as it began to chime, belying the surreal gravity of the moment.

The longer it took my mom to find her words, the more time my mind raced to find the reason I was subpoenaed there. Then realization began to dawn on me, my sister had once again broken her promise. I told her not to say anything to Mom. Why couldn't she keep her word, just one damn time? I only called her because I was terrified. Otherwise, she would be the last person I'd ever confide in. I only had one request: *do not tell Mom*. How hard is it to not torture the woman who birthed you? Michelle's only mission in life seemed to be how much pain she could inflict on Mom. My call to her hadn't even been helpful. I just wanted to know what lynching was.

"Why were those boys so mad at me?" I asked her. "I've never even met them before. Why did they say *my* kind? Whose kind?"

All I heard was silence on the other line. Michelle was never silent. She always had something to say, always used words to hurt others. I thought surely, she'd know what the hell those boys were talking about. Yet, she didn't have one answer for me. Now I had been summoned to Mom's room. Seething, I couldn't wait to tell Michelle off.

As the minutes ticked by in silence, tension filled the room, seemingly kidnapping the oxygen. There was a tightness growing in my own chest that made it hard to breathe normally. Questions were bouncing around in my mind like a runaway rubber ball. Why was what those boys said having such a detrimental effect on her? My mother had never once backed down when it came to her kids. She was fiercely protective of us. Fear was not an emotion my capable mother did well. Yet here she was looking almost panic-stricken. My sister was such a drama queen; I imagined she had told Mom that eminent death was looming around the corner for me.

Wait, is that why she couldn't meet my eyes? Does my mother know something I don't? Do those boys have that power? After what seemed like an eternity, I heard her take in one last, slow, deep breath. She opened her mouth to speak. The words somehow caught in her throat as if her vocal cords refused to perform. Too overwhelming to fit in her mouth, the words stayed lodged in place. She took another drawn-out breath, which sounded muffled, like she was holding one of Grandma's hand-stitched handkerchiefs over her mouth. Her second attempt found more success. At least I heard sounds uttered, but they weren't actually words.

Confusion clouded my thinking. I've seen this woman, holding an infant baby with a four-year-old at her side, stand down a wild bear in the middle of forested land. Never once flinching. We were out picking berries for the pies she promised to bake us that afternoon. My sister had stayed back at the house; she hated scrubbing off the berry stains left on her hands from the tedious work. I had absently strayed too far from my mother, disobeying her insistence to stay close by.

"We aren't the only ones who love wild berries," she had warned me.

But I was four and curious. I was mesmerized by the sky, it was almost turquoise it was so blue, not a cloud to be seen. The bear came out of nowhere, her cub carelessly darting in and out of the bushes. They were foraging. I probably startled them with my litany of lullaby songs as only a four-year-old can belt out. I was closest to the cub when it paused to gaze at me. It took my mom several minutes (or at least that's how it felt to me) to reach the place I stood, frozen.

My mom kept hissing in a whisper as she slowly closed the distance between us.

"Do not move Barbara Lynn. Do *not* move!" she said as she inched toward me.

Once she reached me, she pushed my small body behind her, holding fiercely to my arm. She was cradling my tiny baby brother in her other arm, the basket of berries she once held, long since forgotten. I felt her trembling body stiffen when mama bear began to rise on her hind legs. My face partially shielded by her skirt, I saw the mama bear pause. The silent exchange between the two mothers was unmistakable. My mom never took her eyes from that bear. Another eternal moment passed, then the bear miraculously lowered herself back down to all fours, made a loud sound in the direction of her cub, turned, and ran in the opposite direction.

Suddenly, the words came out in a hurried whisper, falling over themselves like runaway dominoes. They were almost too soft for my ears to understand them.

"Jim is not your father."

But I did hear them. Although I did not comprehend them.

What. Did. She. Just. Say? No other words form in my mind.

The clock was chiming again or maybe it never stopped. Maybe time had suspended itself. As kids, we used to play freeze tag, forced to hold whatever position we were in when tagged.

This was how I felt.

Frozen. Then, something clicked inside my mind and I replayed her words. *Did she just say Jim is not my father?* Rocketing forward, fueled by a lifetime of denial; a lifetime of lies, was just one thought.

This time, that thought refused to be ignored.

Well, who in the hell is? I thought but did not give voice to. No words actually escaped my lips.

"*Jim doesn't want you! No one wants you! You're adopted!*" Michelle's words screamed in my head. Years of her torment.

I still said nothing.

Down the hall, the clock signaled the quarter hour. *Will someone shut that damn thing up?*

I heard the swamp cooler switch on. *It's damn near November, why is it still so hot? Why did we move here? This is a godforsaken town. Some kind of never-ending Twilight Zone episode.*

My mind was in a free-falling tailspin. I felt myself losing grip on the present moment.

The tilt-a-whirl ride came to mind. Last summer, my cousins Kim, Leah, and I were strapped into our respective standing spots on the fair ride. It promised to spin so fast that cylindrical gravity would hold us in our places, as it spins and tilts to and fro.

My world is tilting. Only this time the stage trick removed the floor.

The promise was the same.

You will not fall. The physical laws of gravity will protect you. Did my mother believe that the law of a mother's love would also protect me? From whom was she protecting me?

Still spinning.

"*Your skin is dirty! No one loves you! One night we're all gonna leave you!*" Her words so painful, the only defense was numbness.

The memories kept crashing down on my head like relentless waves beating on the shore. The years of torment, of ridicule, the threats of abandonment. When did my mom protect me from her daughter's abuse? When did she protect me from all the years of taunts and bullying? Did she ever notice the bruises left by Michelle?

And yet, somewhere in the back of my head I know it's not entirely fair. I never told my mother. I never told anyone. Never uttered a word of the hate my sister gave.

"Do you know what we do to people like your kind?" The question from yesterday repeats itself like a vinyl album rutted with scratches.

My kind.

I am spinning.

My kind!

"You don't look like any of us! We don't want you! Do you hear me? You're not wanted."

"Jim is not your father."

As comprehension began to set in, my face needed permission to set the emotions free. I have spent so much of my life protecting my mother. My first memories are of yelling and crashing sounds of breaking glass. All I ever wanted was to save my mom. Another disagreement turned nuclear and wills collided with destructive fury. The emotions were volatile like ticking bombs primed for detonation. There is a tension that hums like white noise in violent families. It's always just below the surface. The wrong uttered words or slightest infraction are powerful enough to trip the wire. The life of people tiptoeing around each other. I don't know when the abuse started, I do know it was hidden, until it wasn't.

Before I had the language to articulate it, I wanted to protect my mother from it. No one ever tasked me with this, I simply assumed the role. When she finally left, maybe I thought I no longer needed to protect her, that I was free. Only I was wrong. I was hardwired and when

Michelle's teenage rebellion turned hostile, I resumed my self-appointed role as protector. How can I protect her now when she has been the one lying to me all these years?

"Jim is not your father."

The swamp cooler switched on and I felt the sensation of the faint breeze on my bare shoulders. It brought me present to my seat across from my mom. I am surprised to feel my tank top clinging to my damp skin. Had I been sweating? Was that a visceral reaction to traumatic news? I watched her face, noting her fear. She was anticipating my reaction. We have been close, she and I. Surviving the teen years, battle worn but not broken. I know my mother treasures our relationship. She had been scarred by her tumultuous relationship with my sister. Michelle's anger seemed to always simmer just below the surface, just add water and you have a raging inferno. Michelle is not Jim's biological daughter, yet her behavior was as close to a DNA match that I know of. I am different though. I am not fueled by anger. I have always just wanted to fit in, to be included, to be accepted. To have peace.

"Do you know what we do to people like your kind?" The memory of the boy's words reminded me, however, that I am always an outsider.

"I was young," my mom began. Shaky at first, then my silence gave her courage, and she quickened the pace.

"I had a six-year-old daughter. I lived at home with all of my family. Grandma and Papap managed a small motel near our house. I worked there helping to clean the rooms and prep for new guests to arrive. It wasn't much, but we did our best to make it nice. It was a hard job. Michelle was already showing all the negative effects of being spoiled rotten by all my siblings, aunts, and uncles. Your grandfather, Papap, adored her like no other. Maybe he was making up for the fact that Michelle didn't have a father around. Either way, she was a brat. Relentless about getting her way all the time. It was exhausting. I was exhausted. I was also very lonely."

"He was in a band. He was the drummer, actually. They would come to town and play the local clubs. After Michelle would go to sleep. I'd leave to go see his band play. I grew up in Detroit and on Motown. We'd go see all the performers live at the Apollo. Little Stevie, The Temptations, The Supremes, oh, how I loved Diana Ross. I missed those times. I missed my life back home. I didn't have any real friends here in California. So, I'd go see his band play. After his sets, he'd sit with me and we'd talk. He was so nice and easy to talk to. He listened. We talked for hours..." She trailed off and after a few moments; I think she said all she was willing to say.

Then, "It just happened. I didn't plan it. His band was staying at the motel, and..." another trail off.

I waited her out.

"I was dating Jim at the time. But this man was so different, and Jim was so hotheaded. Worse than even your Uncle Frank. They were friends, you know."

I didn't know, actually.

"It was late 1969, the lottery of '69 for the Vietnam War was still dragging on. Jim had been drafted and now wanted to get married."

Another long pause.

"Two weeks before we were to be married, I found out I was pregnant with you. I didn't know..." her voice turned soft and unsure of itself.

She swallowed hard, trying to steady herself. Her shoulders surrendered forward, caving as if waving a white flag of defeat. Her silent tears abandoned all pretense of valor. She willed herself to continue. Her eyes looked drawn and somehow the bright green color had dulled. She was battle worn. Her brow furrowed into what looked like a permanent new etching of wrinkles. My mom's sorrow has aged her ten years, right in front of my eyes. The burden of everything she has carried for eighteen years appears to have doubled in size. How many years had she prayed this moment would never arrive?

I felt powerless to help this runaway train correct course. These decisions were made long before my entrance into the world and yet the Italian Catholic guilt I was raised with rose to the surface. Instinctively, I wanted to reach out and comfort my mom. I wanted to take her pain away, tell her not to worry. This woman who has given so much for her family, her whole life.

I said nothing. I did nothing.

Her voice was soft again, almost a whisper:

"I didn't know. Not until you were born. I never told anyone..."

They're all fragments, jumbled together as if I should have understood. As if the story is complete. But it is not and I don't. Maybe it's the look on my face this time that forces her to finish what she was desperately trying not to say.

"My father wouldn't have ever understood. You know how Papap is, he was worse before. He wouldn't have ever understood...

"Not with a Black man..."

The scene in the Matrix when Neo notices the black cat cross his path twice and calls it déjà vu flashes in my mind.

What. Did. She. Just. Say? I am Black???

Did she just say I am Black??

CHAPTER 6

To truly understand someone, you must know their past.

Born in 1922 and 1924, respectively, my grandparents (my mother's parents) were both products of abusive families. Their foundation of the family unit was modeled by parents who were highly dysfunctional themselves. My grandparents grew up in environments where alcoholism, abuse, gambling, and abandonment ran rampant. My mom was raised by two people who, in turn, did the best they could to provide for and raise six kids of their own. While they committed no physical abuse nor became alcoholics, they were also not demonstrative people. My mother and her five siblings did not receive hugs and "I love yous" or "We are so proud of yous." Instead, love was demonstrated by providing housing, food, and education. My grandparents were too locked in survival mode to offer much more. They could not give what they did not have. Until grandchildren that is.

When my mom was eleven years old, her mother had a nervous breakdown. My grandmother emotionally collapsed under unrelenting financial burdens, the weight of being a mother of six, a wife to a demanding husband, and chronic ridicule and verbal abuse from her live-in mother-in-law. Unable to cope, the once very capable and outspoken woman surrendered speaking and retreated to her bedroom, powerless to get out of bed for months.

It took even longer for her to regain her strength to begin parenting and taking care of the home again. No one ever spoke about this. The family simply moved along as if nothing was wrong. As if their silence would repair my grandmother's mental undoing. No one ever discussed the cause and they certainly never sought the help of a psychologist.

The "headshrink doctor," were my grandmother's words, often devaluing an entire mental health profession, "is not welcome here."

My grandparents were born into a time when needing help from a doctor of any kind was a sign of weakness. Growing up during the greatest economic crisis explains that mindset. The weak did not survive during the devastating Depression era.

As the oldest girl, the responsibility fell to my mother. There was never a question about it. It didn't matter that she had only just aged into double digits. She was expected to place her young shoes in her mother's giant footsteps and bear her mother's burden. Unable to care for themselves and without their mother, my mother's younger siblings now depended on her. Changing diapers, cooking, cleaning, and caring for her mother became the daily activities that galvanized her life. For her part, my mom did as she was expected. Maybe it was this event that set my mother on a trajectory seeking approval around every corner and making choices that would never serve her. Maybe it was knowing this fact about her that prevented me from hating my mother for her betrayal.

Shortly after her eighteenth birthday in November, my mother's father was unable to continue working at the Ford factory in Detroit due to his chronic respiratory illness. The doctors said the brutal Michigan winters had taken a severe toll on his health and what he needed was the dry heat weather that California and Arizona offered. My grandparents chose Southern California. The day after school let out the following June, all six siblings, three-year-old Michelle, and my grandparents loaded up a caravan of four cars and a truck to make the cross-country trek to Garden Grove, California.

The move to California ushered in a different life for my family. After all, it was the seventies now. The year of 1970 began a new decade, the sixth year of the Vietnam War, and the end of the Beatles. Diana Ross performed her farewell tour with the Supremes to begin her solo career. Motown was thriving, and NASA's Apollo 13 was forced to abort its moon landing. Widespread, large anti-Vietnam War protests raged across the country and 210,000 of the 750,000 US postal employees walked out on strike. The United States promoted its first two female generals and President Richard Nixon signed the Voting Rights Act Amendments lowering the voting age to eighteen. The national minimum wage was one dollar and sixty cents and a gallon of milk cost sixty-six cents.

Six months settled in Southern California with her family, my mom became a keypunch operator. There was a great demand for keypunch operators at that time as the demand for information grew. My mother needed a trade and her parents invested in what they believed was a respectable career. They sent my mom to a keypunch vocational school. A keypunch operator is exactly what it sounds like. Prior to the advent of computers storing information, keypunch machines were devices designed to precisely punch holes into stiff paper cards at specific locations as determined by keys struck by an operator. The keypunch's accompanying punched cards were then used for data and program entry. The cards were fed into mechanical devices such as adding machines and tabulators that read the keyed information.

By twenty years old, she worked full-time as a keypunch operator during the day. At 5:00 p.m., she would come home to take care of Michelle and begin preparing dinner for her family of eight and a half. Finally, she would drag herself at night to the motel and help her mother and sisters clean motel rooms in the Cloud 9 motel my grandparents managed. Michelle was four years old and showing definite signs of being more than a handful. By all family accounts, Michelle had earned the title of brat. Entitled for her ill-tempered, spoiled, and bad behavior.

To make matters worse, all my mom's six siblings and both of her parents doted on Michelle's every desire. Michelle rarely had to endure "No" for long. As a typical four-year-old, she mastered the art of negotiation and timing. If one family member said no, there was always another victim close by to manipulate a yes. As an astute student of adult reactions, Michelle quickly learned the effectiveness of tantrums. My mother's younger siblings hated witnessing Michelle's outbursts, so they were easy prey. Even at this very young age, Michelle's intelligence was unquestioned, and she skillfully ruled over her subjects and domain with precision beyond her years. For her part, my mom was becoming powerless to control her daughter's behavior. In Germany, they refer to such children as Satansbraten. I can imagine as a single, full-time working mom burdened with full-time evening responsibilities, that my mother began to think of her noxious little nipper resembling something roasting on a spit in hell.

Life for Sandy was a constant monotony of working, cooking, cleaning, and failed attempts at disciplining her child. Adding insult, she was lonely. Leaving Michigan had robbed her of her cousins and her best friends. Being new to town, she hadn't made any friends yet. Each day became the replica of the day before. Rinse, then repeat. Over and over again. She began to feel hopeless and that her dream of happily marrying and having her own house and family was beginning to fade. She was still young in her heart, but the fatigue was taking its toll on her body. After all, it was 1970 and the concept of being an "old maid" was still a widely held belief. Unmarried at twenty years old with a child and living with her family did nothing to diminish her fears. For his role, her father, a traditional Italian father, reminded her constantly that she wasn't getting any younger and that spinster status was fast approaching.

Cleaning rooms in the Cloud 9 motel was arduous. She hated doing it, but knew she'd never complain. Several of the forty-six rooms were occupied with long-term residents. A relatively small property afforded multiple run-ins. That's how they met.

Don had beautiful, brown, smooth skin, the color of toasted cinnamon. Strong muscles defined by physical labor. Arresting brown eyes hooded under thick brows and chiseled cheek bones framed his heart-shaped face. He resembled a Samoan warrior.

At first, it was an occasional hallway pleasantry exchanged, then brief conversations about his band. He was the drummer for a local funk band. She'd grown up on Motown, being a proper Detroit girl. He wasn't from around there, so he'd been staying in the motel gigging and hopeful for the band's big break. Their conversations deepened and a friendship ensued. She made frequent excuses to spend more time at the motel. Often going to see his band play.

It was never supposed to happen. He was married. He had children at home with his wife. It was lonely on the road. The chemistry was undeniable. He was kind and listened to her, really listened. Racism continued to rage throughout the country and in her family. Her parents would never understand. They'd never approve. And yet, he was her safe place. Her secret place.

Frank, Sandy's brother, younger by only eighteen months, was the spitting image of their father, Angelo. Frank bore all the Italian male physical features, dark deep-set eyes, bushy eyebrows, a prominent Italian nose, and dark hair with a respectable wave. The eighteen-month age difference was inconsequential. Frank and Sandy were as close as siblings could be. Growing up, if ever there was a fight with one there was a fight with both. The other notable Italian trait Frank possessed was his hotheadedness. Decades later, during family gatherings often us kids would hear the tales when Sandy would be called in to diffuse a "Frank" situation. She was the only person Frank would ever listen to. She could equal his stubbornness like no other. So many times, especially during their teen years, she was the one who talked him down from the "ledge" and could make him see reason. "His anger would flash and up went the fists. Your Uncle Frank stayed ready for a fight," my mom would often say.

Everything changed when Frank introduced my mom to James Chandler, known to his friends as Jim. Jim, originally from a small rural town in Utah, had moved following after his own sister. Tall, sandy blonde, and good looking, he was Southern California ready. Jim's niece worked at the full-service gas station where Frank had just been hired. She introduced the two and they became fast friends. Frank quickly concluded, however, that Jim was fine as long as they were all just friends, but when he wanted to start dating his sister, Frank did his best to put his foot down. Being protective of his sister, Frank knew Jim's character was quasi-questionable. Frank would never stand for anyone mistreating his sister, not on his watch.

"Do *not* date him!" he yelled one night at my mom.

The two had been out drinking, watching Don's band play. Sandy was distracted watching the man she truly wanted but couldn't have, play the drum solo on the song the band was performing. Being his counterpart, Sandy could outmatch Frank's willfulness. Her own obstinance rejected his advice. Frank didn't understand, she rationalized. She was the one miserable at home, not him. She was the one who was twenty-one years old with a four-year-old. And she was the one in love with a man she couldn't have and couldn't tell a soul. A white woman in love with a Black man. Never in her family.

All Sandy had ever wanted was a family of her own to love and to be loved unconditionally in return. She knew that Jim wanted to get married and she saw him as her way out. An escape from her feelings for Don. An escape out of her monotonous life of constantly trying in vain to please everyone and failing desperately. There was no pleasing her parents. No matter how hard she tried, no matter how "good" she was, it was never enough. So despite Frank's warning, she ran impetuously headfirst into that inevitable collision course of a marriage.

Later, my mom would say all the warning signs were there; she was just so lonely and desperate to get out of her parents' house she ignored them all. She said she believed Jim would change over time. He did not. She had dated Jim for a few months trying to forget Don. Then the US Army claimed Jim's freedom and he was drafted and sent to Vietnam. July was miserably hot and she was lonely. Don was there. It was just one last time, she told herself.

Then Jim's tour ended early and he was suddenly home from the war and wanted to get married. Two weeks before the wedding, she found out she was pregnant with me. She never told me how she felt during her pregnancy, but I assume she spent nine months worrying about my paternity. I can imagine the long nights she would have spent wringing her hands picking the thumb skin, lost in all the what-ifs. She married a white man and could be having a Black man's baby.

On April 13, the following year, I was born on the passenger side of Jim's two-seater car on the way to the army base hospital. Honestly, it was the last thing I've ever been early to in my life. My mother had been wearing a long dress that day. Often, in the retelling she'd reveal that she was afraid to lift the skirt for fear I wasn't breathing. I hadn't made a sound when she pushed me out onto that bucket seat. She had been alone in the car; Jim had already haphazardly parked and bolted into the hospital yelling for a doctor. I wonder though, did she also fear what color my skin would be?

Growing up, my mother often told me the story of how she was so certain I was a boy that she only picked out one boy name. When I was born a girl, the nurse informed my mom that she couldn't leave the hospital without a name. So as a last minute thought, she gave me her mother's name, Barbara. I was born Barbara Lynn Chandler.

CHAPTER 7

I woke up the next morning believing a lie. Then the floodgates burst open and I remembered my mother's words. There was nothing to restrain the questions. The demands. They were like hot iron brands fresh from the fire, designed to burn, dangerous if handled carelessly.

I am Black? What does that even mean? How did I never know? What will change? Will my family treat me differently? Will they love me less? I have grown up witnessing their racist remarks, opinions, and behavior. What will all of this mean now?

It was two weeks since my mother's revelation. I wasn't sure how I knew how much time had passed, everything seemed upside down and inside out. Hours felt simultaneously like days and seconds, like some scene out of *Alice in Wonderland* (Johnny Depp's more psychedelic version). I walked around in what felt like fog so heavy, its burden of weight condemning me. I spent hours laying on my bed in my room. I stared up at the ceiling and only felt numb. Everything I believed was a lie.

Jim. His name brushed the edges of my thoughts. As if on cue, the black and white image of my birth certificate flashed in my mind. The paper is black and the typing is white. No one in my family has a birth certificate resembling mine. The irony is comical. I nearly laugh out loud. Repeatedly, in my mind over these past days I have seen his name neatly typed under the "father" designated line. James William Chandler father to Barbara Lynn Chandler.

"Jim is not your father," my mother had said.

I had not been back to school yet; Art choosing instead to pick up my homework assignments from my teachers. The large manila envelopes sat unopened, littering the top of my desk. I knew what lynching was now, yet the fear elicited from those boys' threats just two weeks ago held no reign over me now. Everything I believed was a lie. I no longer had the emotional bandwidth for their repulsive attempt at intimidating me. Besides, those boys were punks. At 5' 9" and 150 pounds, I'm formidable enough to make abducting me a farfetched idea.

I felt like I was living someone else's life. So surreal. So foreign. It's as if the production crew from *The Twilight Zone* just unloaded in our family room and began a surprise filming. Only I didn't get the script. I don't know what my next line was supposed to be. If I was honest though, I had a deep momentary relief knowing that I no longer had to claim Jim. He was such a bastard.

How was I supposed to feel? Was there some handbook that guided your emotions and directed you to find some inner peace when the woman who has raised you steals your entire identity? Am I supposed to go hide or stand tall? "Black is Beautiful" was a current popular battle cry. But do I have permission to stand under its banner? Historically, one drop of Black blood made you Black. And yet for eighteen years, 50 percent of my blood didn't even command a conversation?

Are Black people just going to welcome me with open arms? Does that even happen? It's been eighteen years and no Black person has ever claimed me. Is there some kind of "by the way, I am Black now" announcement, like some address change notification card you mail to all your friends and family?

Does the fact that when I'm feeling indignant about something, I instinctively roll my neck, make me Black? Literally, not one person in my family does that. Is that just in my DNA? Is that acting Black? Is acting Black even a thing? And how does one act Black? Am I supposed to now go seek out Black friends? I live in Lake Havasu, Arizona, home of the nondiversified. Where on Earth do I find Black folks to befriend?

So many damn questions. They are pervasive, seizing my thoughts mercilessly, like having emotional whiplash. The questions keep me from sleeping, but I don't complain because the nightmares are back. I assume the sheer stress invited them back. I thought those midnight torment shows no longer had the power to imprison me. I thought they were gone forever. I was wrong.

My mom has been on the phone a lot in the past week. Mostly, she takes the calls in her room, but I heard her telling her best friend, Paula (a near second mom to me) that she needed to talk with Lance. I thought that request odd, since Lance is Paula's daughter's boyfriend. What exactly would my mom want with Lance? That answer would come soon enough.

For my part, I spent a lot of time alone, opting to eat dinners isolated in my room. Sitting on my bed for hours, I stared blankly out the window, seeing nothing. The first couple of days were the worst, a torrent of tears.

Tears for that little girl who only ever wanted to fit in, to be the same, to not be dirty. I can see that little girl; I can feel that little girl. But feeling her is dangerous. Feeling her means remembering. And remembering is bad.

Then it happened. That deadened feeling took over. The feeling when you're paralyzed to escape and incapable of screaming. I tried to fight it off, tried telling myself I'm not eight years old anymore, he can't hurt me anymore. That my mom's betrayal is not the same. I don't have to remember. Remembering causes the nightmares. I've been forgetting for all these years. Locked all those memories in a secure tamper-resistant box and buried them in the deep recesses of my mind. I am strong now. This is different.

But the emotions are too close, too raw. I lose the battle and the dam gives way. Unwanted memories crash down like ten thousand tons of water drowning every ounce of fragile sanity I've spent years handcrafting.

———

The room was dark, I'd been in bed for hours, the clear glass jar of pennies laid on its side, ready to ring its alarm if the door opens. When the door opens. I try to believe it will wake me this time. I will hear it this time. I will be ready this time. In my heart, I knew none of this was true.

Fourth grade was when I thought life was going to be better. We had moved to a new neighborhood, but this time I had made a new friend. Life with Michelle had become unbearable. She fought with everyone, ditched school, started using drugs, and would sneak out at night.

My mom would send Art to go find her. She'd come home belligerent. Then she started hanging out with a man ten years older than her; things got much worse.

The fights between Michelle and my mom had gotten pretty bad. I remember over-hearing Mom beg her to agree to an adoption. They argued over this for hours, but Michelle wouldn't budge. I was eight and didn't understand what they were arguing about. I didn't know Michelle was pregnant. I didn't even know where babies came from. These were not conversations had in my house. Eventually, my mother made the decision to send Michelle to Saint Ann's Catholic girl's school. It was run by nuns. What I didn't know was that it was a boarding house for pregnant unmarried teen girls.

I finally felt relief. The house became peaceful. Things were going to be okay from now on. *I had my very own room and, best of all, Michelle no longer lived at home.* How fleeting eight-year-old dreams are. I couldn't have been more wrong. The following January, Michelle moved back home with a baby and a husband.

Lanette was Michelle's baby, so little and frail. She looked exactly like a Kewpie doll. Instantly, I loved this little one, even though she cried incessantly, remedied only by constant holding. If you dared to put her down, her shrill screams could set alarms off. I was certain our neighbors worried about what caused her baby bellows. Instead of her usual cruel treatment, however, Michelle was nice to me. The more I helped with Lanette, the nicer Michelle became.

"I only just turned seventeen," Michelle said, almost begging for my help. I was certain she only said it to guilt me into babysitting. She was exhausted from being up every night with a crying baby. She was desperate, and if being nice to me got her free childcare, well then that's what she'd have to do. For my part, I selfishly wanted a sister who would be kind to me. I did all I could to help. I changed Lanette's diapers, took her out for long walks, and played with her for hours.

While Michelle's reign of terror was over for me, her new husband Jesse's had just begun. It started innocently enough, or so I thought. Just a random stop in my room to "admire it" he said. I was so proud of my new room that I never gave it a second thought. In typical fourth grade fashion, I covered the walls with my school artwork and my favorite comic strip cutouts. My collection of fine alabaster porcelain dolls in their exquisite, fancy lace, eighteenth-century dresses covered the top of my dresser. My small desk in the corner housed the evidence of my allowance for the past two years. Bright pink and white Hello Kitty memorabilia littered every square inch: stuffed Hello Kitty dolls, two coffee mugs, a stapler, and a pair of oversized giant sunglasses all Sanrio branded. I was obsessed.

My favorite piece of the bedroom set was my bed. The honey oak-stained frame sat high up off the floor. It was hand made by Art. He had even used his fancy engraving wood tool to etch a rose in the center of the headboard. A small matching step stool sat unused next to the bed. Mom said I had sprouted up over the past summer, accounting for me not needing the stool anymore. I loved that bed, until I hated it.

The innocent visits became more frequent and then they became increasingly longer. At first, it was just a tremulous hand on my leg, then it inched up to my thigh.

Then it was under the covers. Each night I would wake to see him sitting on the edge of my bed. I was terrified but silent. He wouldn't say anything at first, just sat there like he was admiring something fragile. I was confused. I tried to move away one time, but his hand clamped down viselike on my thigh. I winced in pain, but he didn't release his grip. His eyes burrowed into mine, daring me to say a word. I did not. My mind would reel desperately trying to grasp onto something I could control. I would convince myself I was a shield and "hex" all of my beloved stuffed animals, shielding their eyes so they wouldn't have to witness my torment.

When his hands would find my bare skin and ease under my nightgown, I would feel the numbness take over. My room would become blurry, like how TV shows turn the screen foggy when they are depicting a memory. I would close my eyes; pretend I couldn't feel his fingers pushing my legs apart. My room would disappear, and I would become totally numb. I wouldn't smell his musky cologne I once thought pleasant. I wouldn't feel him force my small hand into his unzipped pants. I wouldn't feel his rough hand over mine rhythmically, forcefully rubbing his throbbing penis until my hand felt something sticky and wet. I wouldn't hear the low groans sounding like wild animal guttural utterances he'd make. I wouldn't feel the tears stinging my eyes and silently streaming down my cheeks like our kitchen windows on rainy days. The sound the mattress springs made when relieved of his weight was my only indication that night's nightmare was over.

Waiting, breath held, I'd count the seconds like a veritable stopwatch, until I was certain he wouldn't be back. Slowly, with hands that barely functioned for the trembling, I'd pull my nightgown back down. My inner thighs would attempt to disobey my command to swing my legs off the side of the bed. The vile taste in my mouth threatened to trigger the vomiting. I knew I had to hurry.

There's not much time. I made the mistake of not listening once before. I tiptoed to the bathroom. In the cold, army green porcelain tub I'd sit naked, violently shivering, my teeth rattling, sounding like a machine gun in my head. The numbness would begin to recede. Knowing the feelings weren't far behind, I needed to wash myself. Try to clean off his stench. My mom only bought Irish Spring soap; normally I hated the bright green, overly fragrant bar, but these nights I was always relieved to see that familiar oblong cake.

I'd turn the water on slowly. Avoiding any loud sound, the water barely streaming out, I'd sob silently into my drawn-up knees covering my bare chest, asking for what felt like the gazillionth time, why?

Why was I so ugly? I heard the priest say one Sunday at mass that God didn't like ugly. Hadn't Michelle screamed it at me for years?

"You're ugly!" Maybe she was right, 'cause clearly God didn't like me either.

———

The insidious memory released its corrupt hold on me and the present moment came back into focus. The fog eventually lifted and I am curled into the familiar fetal position on my bed in Lake Havasu. My body felt the trauma as if it just happened. My teeth gritted together, stomach clenched, and arms wrapped protectively around my body. I took slow deep breaths and began the familiar process of detangling myself, stuffing the nightmares back into their protective box, padlocking them away.

I admonished myself to stay present. I repeated over and over again, "You are safe. No one can hurt you like that anymore. This is different. Mom loves me. She is *not* Jesse."

CHAPTER 8

I knew my mother had become desperate for a solution when she told me I would be moving back to California to live with Lance. Lance was the twenty-two-year-old boyfriend of her best friend's daughter. He rented a house with three of his friends twenty minutes from my old high school. So yes, my otherwise conservative mother was about to allow her not quite eighteen-year-old daughter to move four hundred miles away and live basically unsupervised with four twenty-two-year-old men.

My mother had been outmatched by small town bigotry and had to do something drastic. She couldn't keep her Black daughter in this racist white town and risk the backlash of intolerance. She didn't agree with me living in a bachelor pad, but she was more averse to me being terrorized by the desert locals.

So there I was, three months shy of my eighteenth birthday having just learned of my new blackness, living with the equivalent of four white frat boys. They drank a lot, smoked a lot of weed, and never ate a single healthy meal. They were also kind and protective of me. They shared their food with me when I was out and let me watch TV with them in the living room. A veritable live-in little sister.

My new home was a single-story, beige, ranch-style house with the master bedroom and bath in the back of the property. The entryway was barely noteworthy. You really just walked straight into a large spacious room with vaulted ceilings and a giant picture window that framed the front of the house. The décor inside was typical bachelor pad hodgepodge. The sparse furnishings were a collection of bare-bone essentials. The single window treatment was budget, off-white vinyl blinds missing most of the plastic slats. Two unmatched, faded brown, well-worn couches, a garage sale rescue coffee table with permanent beer bottle rings etched in the wood, and a lamp that only worked when you jiggled the lightbulb. Finally, the pièce de résistance was a massive, ten-year-old, floor model TV that required four antennas—because you can't have a proper bachelor pad without this signature centerpiece.

The second bedroom down the hall was mine, all 150 square feet of it. It fit a compact double-size mattress on a metal frame, a painted wood milk crate masqueraded as a nightstand, and a modest four-drawer chest served as clothes storage. My provisions were random and ill-matched and perfect to me. I shared a bathroom with two of the frat boys. Admittedly, this was my least favorite part of the arrangement. Let's just say cleanliness was not their strength. Disgusting is putting it mildly. I showered with my flip-flops on.

From January until May, Mission Viejo High School recorded very few sightings of me. My attendance was abysmal. In my defense, it was spring in Southern

California, and the frat house was thirty minutes from the beach. I had a car, a babysitting job that didn't start until 3:00 p.m., and hours to fill with anything but school. I was trying my best to pretend that my mother hadn't just rocked my world. I told myself I didn't want to squander all my new unsupervised freedom. Honestly, I was running as fast as I could from the truth. As long as I could keep up my breakneck pace, I figured I could outrun all of it and never look back.

One random Tuesday morning, I decided to grace my teachers with my presence. US Government was second period, (I could never make it on time for first). The teacher was passing out exam papers. He paused at my desk with a quizzical look and sincerely asked if I was a new student. I didn't let the event phase me. I had a secret weapon. I could write and sign my own absent excuse notes. I'd write repeated notes for days at a time, then nonchalantly stroll into class like a genuine prima donna. This was not the world of instant access or cell phones. My parents were in a whole other state. I was on my own. Clearly, too much independence for a newly eighteen-year-old girl.

It was graduation day. Robed in the traditional black graduation cap and gown, my heart was racing and my head pounded from the stress. I felt paralyzed by my own guilt. Although it was a breezy Southern California day, I was in a sweaty panic. Just three days prior, both my English and my History teachers informed me that I wasn't passing their classes. They also made it clear that it was too late to turn in any make-up assignments. They didn't have any mercy on me. And why would they? I don't remember turning in one assignment that spring semester. I clearly demonstrated that I didn't value my education so why should they? I didn't blame them and yet I knew without those passing grades, I wasn't graduating.

The horror of it for me was that my entire family was coming to see me graduate. There were all the Pannos, sitting in the bleachers. They'd have waited for hours fanning themselves in the June heat, if that's what it took to see me cross the stage. They'd spent twelve years anticipating this moment. Giving accolades and money at every positive report card. Never missing an opportunity to reinforce the importance of a high school diploma. Not having a diploma was tantamount to joining the ranks of the homeless in my house. Mine was a blue-collar and mid-management working family who counted on their children to surpass their achievements. Their hopes and their dreams for me rested on me holding up my end of the bargain.

My cousin Tina had already done her part and graduated last year. Not graduating was simply *not* an option. The moment my mother became a teen mom, it was understood that she would have to drop out. The year of 1963 was a different era. Unwed teen girls were punished while the boys weren't forced to endure that shame. My mother was emphatic that I not repeat her mistakes. I knew she was counting on me to succeed, validating her years of sacrifices.

Knowing all of this fueled my panic. Every time I glanced up into the stadium and spotted the clan clustered together, my heart sank a little more. They had no idea. What was I supposed to tell all of them when the principal didn't announce my name into the microphone?

What I would've given to have a second chance. The realization that I had made the biggest mistake of my life hit me hard. This was my education, my life, and instead of using my opportunity, I wasted it as if it meant nothing. I knew better. For years, my mother told me of patriarchal societies around the globe outlawing educating girls. Why had I wasted my chance?

I decided right then and there standing on the steps that if my name was called, I wouldn't waste the grace bestowed upon me. I had dreams. I wanted to be successful. I wanted to do something big in my life. Most importantly, I decided that learning I was half Black wasn't a curse. I was different, yes, but I was also destined for greatness. I resolved that I wasn't going to be a victim, that I wasn't going to let my "difference" define me. Instead, I was going to figure my way out in the world. I didn't know what I wanted as a career, but I did know that whatever it was, my mother had taught me that I could make it happen. Long before Beyonce sang it, my mother had been saying for years that women ruled the world.

The marching band belted out one tune after the other, hoping to inspire school pride and to alleviate some of the boredom as we waited for the ceremony to begin. All of the soon-to-be graduates were positioned to the left of the stage, lined up in alphabetical order and threatened by our vice principal not to move an inch until they were called. This is where I stood, perspiring profusely, barely surviving my repeated panic attacks. Shane Nagel was in front of me and Luanna Oliveria was behind. I kept nervously shifting my weight from my left foot to my right. Apparently, brushing against Luanna one too many times because she finally jerked my arm in annoyance.

"What is wrong with you?" she demanded.

"They aren't going to call my name!" I hissed back at her. It wasn't her fault, but my nerves were frayed.

"What are you talking about? We are here. We've been practicing all week. They will call *all* the names. And yours will be one of them," she said, while rolling her eyes. Luanna wasn't known for her patience.

"You don't understand…" I tried to rebut.

The blare of the band's newest tune drowning out my words. It was okay though because the procession began moving forward and my heart was now near exploding. All of my family, my white family, had driven in for over an hour. They had taken off work to be here at my graduation, celebrating me. Except now I was going to disappoint them. My regret at not taking education seriously welled up inside me. The shame for not being more responsible shortened my breath. The warm summer breeze picked up, and on cue, all the graduates clutched at their caps to prevent them from taking flight. And despite the ample air, my lungs felt compressed. Panic threatened to take over when I felt Luanna's hand on the small of my back ushering me forward. We were near the stage, the principal calling out the graduates' names.

That morning, I saw myself for the first time. The oval, antique, full-length mirror reflected back a young lady with tremendous potential, who hadn't ever truly applied herself. I was an adult now. The realization that my choices now were going to affect the rest of my life hit me hard. This was no longer practice.

"Daylin Myers"

"Shane Nagle"

"Barbara Navarro"

"What?" I exclaimed, thunderstruck at hearing my name.

Luanna was literally pinching my arm, hard. She was smiling at the audience and, behind that grin, growling at me to cross the stage. My feet never touched the floor. I floated over to where our principal stood, his frozen smile in place.

It felt like my name had just been announced as the mega lottery winner. Relief, then joy, then elation rose up and expanded in my heart so completely I actually felt lightheaded. I didn't know how or why, and I didn't know what I did to deserve this miracle. But it was, in fact, a miracle. What I do know is that I was the happiest most relieved graduate on that stage!

In that moment, I made a decision. I decided I would move back to Arizona with my parents and figure out how I was going to turn my life into what I wanted. These past months, I had been smoking cigarettes and smoking weed. Worse yet, I was hanging out with very privileged white kids who had access to their parent's platinum Am Ex credit cards and seemingly unending money. So I joined them snorting cocaine and drinking a lot of Bacardi (don't ask, we probably just thought it sounded fancy). Yet, I didn't want any of that for myself. I knew in this moment that I wasn't taking any of those bad habits into the future I would create for myself. Instead, I was taking responsibility for my life and I was choosing to be happy.

Hearing my name, my family in true Panno style, erupted in cheers. The remainder of the alphabet was called. I don't remember a single name or face. The relief was so complete. My heart beat in gratitude for a blessing I knew I had not earned but was given anyway.

Then it was over, and I was hugging my family and listening to the chatter all around me as the other graduates reunited with their families. Hugs and promises to meet up over the summer were given to my fellow graduates. Then the demands for lunch from the little cousins couldn't be ignored any longer. Life was back on track.

CHAPTER 9

Two weeks after graduation, I had my room all packed up. Armed with a new mindset and renewed sense of purpose, I said goodbye to Lance and the frat boys and made the long six-hour drive back to Lake Havasu, Arizona. Since I had decided that some computer error angel had gifted me with a high school diploma, I wasn't going to waste the blessing. I knew I needed a high school diploma *and* a degree if I was going to realize the success I was destined for. Direct admittance into a university was out of the question. Computer error graduation GPA was good for only one thing. My journey would need to begin at the community college level.

In late June, full of hope and determination, I drove my sporty, white, two-door Ford Escort to the east side of town. My destination, to register at my new academic home for the next two years. I had a plan and I was ready to execute. To set the mood, my speakers were blasting Eric B & Rakim's "I Ain't No Joke." Driving onto Mohave Community College's "campus," I was temporarily crestfallen. I pulled into a dirt parking lot and had to wait nearly thirty seconds for the dust to settle back to the ground before I could open my car door. Sweltering heat accosted me as I got out. It was literally so hot my body responded with goose bumps.

It's 8:15 in the morning! How in the hell is it this damn hot out?

"God, help me," I heard myself whisper.

I grit my teeth. The campus consisted of three mobile home trailers parallel parked in a dirt lot. Three thirty-foot saguaro cacti stood center stage and were bordered with the traditional desert rock garden. A vinyl banner announcing the name of the college served as the marquee.

"*This* is the college?" I asked of no one in particular.

I gave myself a pep talk. Encouragingly, with the most enthusiasm I could muster before 9:00 a.m. I said, "Listen, this doesn't have to be paradise. You just need to enroll and do well in these classes and you can transfer. It's going to be fine."

These mini self-pep rallies would become a staple over the next eighteen months. I was on a mission and if a dirt-lotted, vinyl sign-having, mobile home trailer was the vehicle, then damnit, I'm gonna ride it until the wheels fall off.

I had registered for English 101, Math 010 (essentially remedial math), Psychology 101 (the only course that didn't have a college algebra prerequisite requirement), and Computers 101. I attended classes on Mondays, Wednesdays, and Fridays. Every night, I studied for a minimum of three hours. Every single night. School had never come easy and community college was no exception. It felt like I had to work twice as hard to be half as good.

I also got a job at the new Izod retail shop that was opening in a couple of months. I was scheduled on Tuesdays, Thursdays, and Saturdays. The manager had relocated from their Phoenix store and was on-site to direct the new construction. She was as kind as she was professional. Susan was encouraging to her new employees and ran her stores with skilled efficiency.

My life became very routine. It consisted of attending and studying for my basic general education classes, an undeniable thirteenth grade, and selling golf shirts to the local retirees. Given that no one would've ever accused me of being a dedicated high school student, I was actually relieved at another opportunity to revisit and really learn the material. A young academician I had not been. That was all changing now.

My routine settled into place and something new arose—early morning time with my dad. Before, I would get up, dressed, and fly out the door to class rushing past my dad who was already up with a "Have a good day" over my shoulder. Art had always been an early bird. He loved the quiet hours in the morning. No matter how late he'd go to bed, by 5:45 a.m. you'd find him sitting with his coffee and his thoughts. Since I had to be up early as well, I would walk into the living room each morning to join my dad. We'd sit quietly, him drinking his black coffee with one cream and me with my cream and a dash of coffee. Then we'd share a few moments of weather chitchat or what was happening at the local grocery store he was managing.

My dad was easily my favorite person. He was lean and tall at 6' 2" with a head of thick, black, wavy hair. He had a work ethic that belied his lanky slender frame. His energy could light up a room. His generosity was unmatched. He had an unending love for history, especially the wars. He'd spend hours talking to anyone, and I mean anyone, about anything. I don't think he ever met a stranger in his life. To meet Art is to know you have a loyal friend for life. He never judged. He gave everyone immense grace and expected very little of people in return. He was fair and believed the best about folks. The Beach Boys were his favorite band, but if Motown was playing, he'd never leave the dance floor. James Brown had met his match. I loved this man so deeply.

When he met my mom, she already had three children, ages thirteen, six, and two (I was the six-year-old). He, on the other hand, had never had a child of his own. My mother had told him on their first date that we were a package deal. Jim was completely out of the picture and my mom was on her own. I don't know if Art ever had doubts about becoming an instant father because all we knew was he embraced us kids as his own immediately. They dated for a year before he proposed. He stepped into the role of husband and dad simultaneously unquestioned. He loved us kids with all of his immense heart.

The weekend after they were married in Las Vegas was Mother's Day. As I said, we did family gatherings on every holiday. My mom's brother, Uncle Frank, and his family had just arrived; the rest of the family was still on their way. Uncle Frank and his wife, Aunt Barb, had been the witnesses in the wedding. Uncle Frank, Art, and I were all standing in the garage. Art liked creating with his hands, and he was making a wooden toy train for my little brother. He paused when he realized the planer was sitting on the table next to where I was standing.

"Barbara Lynn, can you hand me the planer please?" he asked.

As I handed him the tool, I instinctively said, **"Here you go, Dad."**

We both looked at each other in surprise. I hadn't planned on saying that, it just came out. I wasn't even sure if it was okay. We had never discussed it before. I stared at him, uncertain for a long, silent moment. What if he didn't want to be called *Dad*? I was in third grade and hadn't called anyone dad since Jim, and that was three years ago when the strangling incident happened. Jim was so mean all the time that he barely seemed to want to be anyone's dad. Yet, he was mine.

What if this man (Art), who was not my "real" dad didn't want me to refer to him as such? My fears must have registered on my face because Art walked over to me, wrapped his arms around me, and whispered into my ear,

"I was wondering when you were going to call me Dad. You are my daughter. I love you and nothing will ever change that."

I buried my face in his chest and cried tears of relief. For the next twenty-eight years, I was honored to call him my dad. Every day he got up and did the job. He taught me that you aren't given your titles, you earn them. I can honestly say that a day doesn't go by that I don't miss my best friend.

The next year passed in a blur of textbooks, classes, studying, peddling golf merchandise, and writing papers until two o'clock in the morning. I actually felt myself getting smarter, as if my brain had been patiently waiting for me to quit driving with the emergency brake on. I worked really hard at school and earned a place on the honor roll. Then, I completely astonished myself earning straight A's and was awarded the dean's list for the next three semesters. Essentially, I reinvented myself into the learner I had never been before. I worked and made a few friends at the college. I did my best to stay focused. My new dream was to gain acceptance into a university and earn my bachelor's degree.

After searching endlessly, taking every personality and aptitude test available, I finally chose a profession. Answering a litany of questions like "If you were on a deserted island, which of the following would you take?" or "What is the word most people would use to describe you?" I decided I want to become an attorney. I had secretly dreamed of becoming a doctor, but since my now infamous candy striping incident when I was thirteen, I don't think I'm allowed back in the hospital, except maybe as a patient.

The training had just ended forty-five minutes earlier when a nurse asked me to assist her. I was only there to support the patient while she changed his colostomy bag. I figured it wasn't my fault, on account of the stench was so putrid. Poor Mr. Jackson. It took the nurse twenty minutes to clean all my vomit off him. So the law it is. Plus, when I discovered that attorneys earn a Juris Doctor degree, I decided I would make my family call me Dr. lawyer.

New York City would be my future home where I'd become a famous attorney. It's almost humorous thinking how polar opposite Lake Havasu City and New York City are. I hung colorful pictures and magazine clippings of high-rise lifestyles on my walls. I was determined to make this my new reality.

Looking back, it's so clear that I was still running, still hiding. I'd yet to have a conversation with my family about my inner turmoil. Never a confession about how confused I was, how lonely I felt. Never a conversation about the emotional rot I'd felt all the years of Michelle's torment over my skin color. How alien I'd been in my own family. And God forbid I admit to anyone about the molestation.

My family members were professionals at denial, and I had learned the skill well. I kept my focus on my future so I could forget my past. I was desperately cocooning myself in the hopes of emerging as an entirely different version of myself. The flaw in my plan: wherever you go, there you are.

Then, when I was nineteen, I landed a job as a hostess in the nicest restaurant in town. Shugrue's Bar and Grill, owned and operated by the Shugrue brothers, Mark and Tim. In a small town, this job was highly coveted and after the placid retail environment, I was elated at the high-end, fast-paced restaurant atmosphere. In my thinking, this was a perfect setting to earn my needed NYC chops. Little did I know that I would never actually make New York my home.

Shugrue's sat high up off the channel shore; its three-story aerial height created the best view in town of the London Bridge. The entire back side of the restaurant facing the bridge was one large atrium. Floor to ceiling crystal clear glass kept pristinely immaculate so as not to diminish the spectacular view. It was a fine dining restaurant with a family atmosphere. Fine dark cherry wood tables and matching low-back chairs created the seating. Hand carved, richly stained bookcases lined the walls housing volumes of classic books. The entrance featured a deep mahogany brown, oversized, ornate wine rack displaying dozens of bottles. Deep hunter green carpet patterned with majestic gold designs lined the floors.

The atrium was my favorite room in the entire building, sixteen tables seated a total of sixty-eight people; every seat was placed to maximize the spectacular view. The deep green carpet added to the elegance of the room. I became an expert daydreamer in that room. It just felt magical to me. I loved working the lunch shifts. The waitstaff would arrive just after the kitchen staff to prep early each morning. After all my duties were complete and before we opened, I'd go into the atrium and stand at the glass wall to gaze down at the brilliant water. Its rhythmic motion was mesmerizing. In the distance beyond the bridge and the channel, the lake opened up into its massive fullness. From my vantage point, I could see the harsh craggy, red rock Mohave Mountains, void of any vegetation, reign in the vast lake narrowing it before its reentry into the Colorado River.

The hues of the blues and greens, sparkling like diamonds dancing on the surface of water. At the shoreline, the water lapped against the sand like a constant game of keep-away.

The early morning shoppers milled around in the specialty boutiques below. Occasionally, on my morning shifts, I'd watch young children squeal and splash in the water alongside their vacationing families, their boats buoyed nearby. Everyone looked so happy. I'd spend my time imagining how perfect their lives were, never burdened by family secrets or painful identity crises that questioned their worthiness.

Maybe, my still-teenage mind understood that everyone experienced pain and that family secrets were not unique to my family. I was only sure of one thing; although outwardly I appeared functionally calm, inside I was coming apart at the seams.

"God, help me," I heard myself whisper.

CHAPTER 10

Phone calls change lives. On a boring Sunday afternoon, everything changed... again. The phone rang while I was sitting at the dining room table, elbows deep in Biology 102 (not my favorite subject). I was desperately attempting to decipher why Fick's Law of Diffusion was not the same as osmosis. My head immersed in cell transport, I ignored the grainy trill rings at first, figuring someone else would grab it. My mom was in the sunroom she commissioned my dad to build to house her enormous plant collection, and I forgot there's no phone in that room.

To know Sandy is to know she possesses ten green thumbs, and they require an outlet. Plants were my mother's love language and she was fluent in every dialect. The sunroom's walls were painted a light baby yellow to reflect all the window light that poured in. Floor to ceiling, the sunroom was the domicile to over one hundred plants large and small. Large macraméd plant holders she had hand woven, hung from the ceiling with bright green leafy vines spilling over the top like nature-designed chandeliers. Dozens of dainty, frilly doilies hand crocheted, lay supporting decorative pots on the various shelves.

It was like walking into a rainforest, every shade of green wildlife, from flowering succulents to lush perennials, greeted you. It was her favorite room in the house, and she'd spend hours of her free time potting and repotting, tenderly coaxing the potential out of any seedling.

Years later, when I had my own house, I remember Art pretending to be the voice of the potted plants my mom would gift me.

"Help me! Save me!" he'd exclaim in what was supposed to be a terrified plant voice. "Don't leave me with her! You know I'll never make it out alive! I'm a dead plant walking!" No one laughed harder than me. I had inherited none of my mother's gardening savvy.

My parents were the epitome of DIYers. They would've put Chip and Joanna Gaines to shame. Raised by frugal post-Depression parents, Sandy learned if she wanted something, she had to do it herself. The twenty-three-year-old Detroit-raised city girl found herself on a farm in rural Utah with barely any indoor plumbing, not a problem. Without YouTube or Google, she became a master gardener and farmer in less than a year, postpartum by the way.

I don't think I ever witnessed my mom say, "Oh, I can't do that." It just wasn't in her vocabulary. I also don't think Art had any idea who he was up against when he committed to his nuptials. My mother roped him into all, and I do mean *all*, of her ideas. She wanted a new bookshelf; Art can build it. She wanted to rip up the carpet and strip the one-hundred-year-old, half-rotted wood floors, Art can do it. She wanted a sunroom with two walls of ginormous windows, Art can do it. And he'd do it too.

Granted, the concrete floor collected puddles of the overrun water after every plant-watering day because Sandy wanted a storage closet added at the last minute during buildout. Art, demonstrating his true lack of general contracting skills, did the best he could. Dad and I giggled every time we were in the room, which probably explained why Mom never let us in.

After the third ring, I dragged my attention from procaryotes and eucaryotes to answer the phone.

An unfamiliar voice asked, "Is this the home of Sandra Panno?"

This was odd, given that was my mom's maiden name. She hadn't been a Panno in nearly twenty years. I ignored the slight oddity because the phone voice sounded so sincere and if I could pinpoint it, a little nervous.

"Yes, this is her home," I responded. "How can I help you?"

"I'd like to speak with her. I mean, if you don't mind," said the female voice. She had a soft warm voice, albeit nervous.

"Of course. This is her daughter. Can I help you?"

I inquired again. I knew my mom would be irritated at me for disturbing her coveted sunroom time. Long pause.

"Uh, no. No, I need to speak directly to her please." Still soft, her voice was determined now.

Something in her tone told me this was a conversation my mom needed to have.

"Sure, I'll go get her."

At first my mom took the call in the kitchen where I had answered it. But within a minute she looked directly at me, and told me to hang up once she had picked it up in her room. It was odd because my mom's voice was always sure of itself. That directive came out shaky. Her eyes, however, answered my question and I dared not inquire further.

Two hours later, my mom called for my dad. She hadn't once come out of her bedroom. The fundamental life of molecules had long since lost my attention. I kept peering down the hallway, expecting my mom to emerge. Nearly ninety more minutes passed after my dad went inside. Now all of my senses were on high alert. Something was wrong, but for the life of me, I didn't know what.

Eyes red and swollen, my mom allowed my dad to lead her to our living room couch. My face must have shown my confusion because my dad simply shook his head indicating that I say nothing. The living room was only for formal company and holiday adult card games. It was the one room in the house us kids, yes, at nineteen I am still considered a kid, are not allowed. Decorated in my mom's prized antique furniture, the room was formal and immaculate. The deep mahogany wood shelves and accented furniture oiled to a polished shine. Dainty porcelain knickknacks lay on the hand-carved end tables. Her grandmother's delicate China displayed behind the cabinet glass doors, both handed down for three generations.

My dad had sat her in the middle of the cushioned antique couch. He positioned himself next to her. Ever since I had known this man, this was his place. Always by her side, supporting her no matter what. I loved him so much in that moment. I had seen this woman endure violence at the hands of Jim. Witnessed the drunken verbal assaults. Watched her beg for her life, her hands desperately trying to unclench his hands from around her throat because Jim had her up against the kitchen wall again. The dinner he had refused to come in for thirty minutes earlier was cold.

Art was everything Jim had been incapable of being. Art was loyal and dedicated to my mom. As such, she leaned on him both emotionally and physically. She placed her head on his shoulder, her face puffy, back stiff, hands in her lap. She was wringing them again. My dad's hands lay on top of hers, but I recognized the familiar picking motion of her fingers. My stomach immediately clenched. The grandfather clock chimed down the hall, and the irony was not lost on me. But then she smiled. She looked up at me and smiled. I looked to my dad and he was smiling too. I was so taken aback, I just smiled back.

Were we supposed to be smiling?

My mom began, "I have something to tell you."

"That phone call was from a young woman named Laura." She began. "When I was your age, before Grandma and Papap moved us to California, I was engaged."

This I had never known. I felt my jaw drop open and my dad's eyes bore into me to remain silent. I think he feared that if interrupted, my mom wouldn't tell the story. I learned later that forty-five of those ninety minutes spent in the room together was him convincing her to tell me.

She continued, "I had met a young man and fell in love. When Papap announced we were relocating, I was devastated. I wanted to marry this young man. Then I found out I was pregnant. Michelle was two years old, and life was already really hard with her. I knew my mother would never allow another baby. So the young man and I made a plan. I would help make the drive to California; there were eight of us, four cars and a truck. Everyone was needed and I was expected to help. The trek across the country was brutal; it was July, extremely hot and the cars didn't have air conditioning. The younger kids needed to be settled so they could start the school year in their new schools. I was in the throes of morning sickness and first trimester fatigue, pulling over to vomit was a frequent occurrence."

"Finally, the journey ended, and we got resettled into our new home. Everything was so foreign in California. Palm trees and the beaches were brand-new sites. The move was expensive and getting jobs was required. Your Uncle Frank and I brought our paychecks home to help support the family, and Papap gave us a weekly allowance. It was enough for gas, cigarettes, and a little spending money. That was no different than in Michigan. That's just what families did. There was never a question about it."

"After I had saved up enough money, I flew back to Michigan. I was devastated when I returned. The young man had been sleeping with several other girls in my absence. Heartbroken, I boarded a plane back to California. My mother, after finding out, laid down the law. She explained that I was nineteen with a three-year-old and no skillset. There were eight people living in our three-bedroom, one bath house and there were more days than money. She decided that I was to give this baby up for adoption. She told me my sacrifice would offer the baby a better life than what I could provide."

I knew my mom had spent her whole life seeking her parent's affection and approval. So without question, I knew that she had done exactly as her mother had instructed. I also knew that all my mom ever wanted was a family of her own to love and to be loved unconditionally. An unconditional love she hadn't felt growing up. She did not give voice to the agony she felt after giving birth and leaving the hospital with empty arms and breasts full of milk. But her pain was evident. She never cried while retelling her tale, maybe she had done enough of that already. Twenty-one years later, however, the anguish in her words induced a deep sorrow in my own heart. My mother had endured so much in her life; I longed to unburden her from her grief.

"Her name is Laura. She is twenty-one years old. She lives in Irvine, California. She was adopted by a couple who already had two boys and wanted a girl. She has had a good life and seems like a very nice young woman." My mom trailed off.

I wasn't sure if the conversation was over.

Do I say anything? What do I say? Do I hug her? Stay in my own chair?

Finally, I uttered, "Do we get to meet her?"

My mother exhaled and smiled. Her relief was palpable. I realized then that she had been holding her breath, worried about my reaction. About how I would respond. It hadn't been eighteen months since she had upended my life with her previous revelation. Maybe she anticipated this would be the event that would send me over the edge. That I would feel betrayed.

She was wrong. My stomach was still shaky, but deceived I did not feel. What I felt was relief. Those hours while she was in her room, I had incessantly paced, made a snack, left it uneaten, paced some more, and imagined the worse. I worried about the inevitable demolition this unknown caller was about to have on our family.

So I actually have two sisters. It may seem odd, but to hear I had another sister gave me hope. I wasn't struck with anger or sadness or betrayal. Instead, I hoped for the sister I could never find in Michelle. Mom said Laura sounded like a lovely woman. I doubt anyone had ever used "lovely" to describe Michelle.

It would be months before we met Laura and learned that she lived just ten minutes from where my mom worked for ten years, and she was a senior when I was a freshman and our high schools played each other in sporting events, and she was about to graduate USC and I was about to transfer to USC. Yes, relief is what I felt.

I couldn't have known then that meeting Laura would jar me to my core. My mother had four children. Each of us with different fathers, yet the only one she gave up was her very own mirror image. Laura possessed all the physical likeness to my mom, a mother she did not grow up calling as such; a mother I did, a mother I bore only the faintest resemblance to.

CHAPTER 11

Written twenty-five years earlier, *The Autobiography of Malcolm X* found its way into my hands during a trip to Sedona, Arizona. The Shugrue brothers owned a second restaurant in Sedona where Mark lived. During Tim and Jackie's annual week vacation, Mark managed both restaurants and chartered a Cessna 170 plane to shorten the nearly four-hour drive between the two cities. That year, Mark had invited Cindy and I to travel with him on his day trip to Sedona.

Cindy is another hostess I had been working with at Shugrue's for about a year. Her dry humor was hilarious, and I really liked her. She never looked down at me or judged me. Her ability to laugh at herself without any pretense endeared her to me. On super busy weekend nights, the kitchen would stack the to-go orders on the countertop behind the hostess station. Shugrue's was famous for their spicy chicken fingers. They were also our favorite thing on the menu. When no one was watching, Cindy and I would nip into the Styrofoam containers and steal a finger or two. I can't tell you how many full to-go orders our stealthy fingers turned into half orders.

Mark said we could tour Sedona and then meet him for a late lunch and we'd fly back before sunset. My elation at the invite was contagious; neither Cindy nor I slept the night before. I felt like a five-year-old waiting on Santa. What I didn't know then was that trip would trigger a seismic rift in my life that I would never recover from.

We departed shortly after sunrise, the sun rays giving birth to a brand-new day. At thirteen-thousand-feet altitude, flying through those red rock mountains in that tiny plane was the most beautiful scenery I had ever experienced. Mesmerizing rusty red mountain hues juxtaposed the stunning golden desert sandstone canyons. Among some of the oldest rocks on Earth, estimated to be over two billion years old, the river-formed canyons display a millennia of rock minerals parading lustrous golds and fiery reds. The pilot maneuvered the small aircraft, alternating dropping the right wing then the left so we didn't miss a thing. Spellbound, I peered through my backseat window down into the vast chasm of unrestrained beauty. My eyes both feasted and starved at the same time. All I could think is, this is how God brags.

Cindy and I began our day with a wet adventure seven miles north of the town. Slide Rock is a famous eighty-foot-long, four-foot-wide slippery rockslide. Nature formed it from a little brook flowing through a narrow chute of smooth sandstone. Algae on the rocks and a 7 percent decline from top to bottom creates the slippery ride. It's nestled between an apple orchard and surrounded by the red rocks of Sedona's Oak Creek. The slide down was so much fun, we were like two six-year-olds at Disneyland.

After the water adventures and with beach towels wrapped around our waists, Cindy and I perused the local boutiques in the quaint downtown. Lazily meandering through the local used bookstore, I paused at a sign indicating an African American section, ironically (or not) located in the back of the store. The African American sign felt more like it read: "For Black eyes only. Everybody else: nothing to see here." I was equally grateful and offended. I was impressed that this nondiverse town had an African American section. At the same time, I was dismayed that Black authors were restricted to a section that otherwise implied their appeal was only to Black readers. Newly Black, I followed the sign to the back of the store. That sign was about to change my life.

Propped up at eye level, I met Malcolm X's gaze staring out from the cover. Mesmerized, I picked up the paperback. The bottom right corner showed frayed edges and several of the top corners had been turned down, indicating the previous owner's habit of bookmarking their place. *The Autobiography of Malcolm X* was a fat paperback that felt ominously heavy in my hands. As if the searingly painful words contained on the 466 pages weighted the book down.

Cindy and I met up at the front of the store and when she headed out to leave, I made some excuse about needing to pee and headed back inside, alone. Nearly a year had passed since my mom's lie had been exposed. An inner conflict had taken up residence in my gut. I found myself cringing any time race was brought up. It was 1991—racism and bigotry raged on in this country, so it was inescapable. The topic may have become unavoidable, but I had become skillful at ducking and dodging it. Also, a recent and unwelcome phenomenon was emerging. It felt like, without me divulging it, the world somehow got my mom's memo and wanted my opinion about being Black, as if I even had a clue. Random white strangers walked up to me and said, "Black is beautiful."

Or in a class discussion, I would suddenly be called on to speak about race. As if somehow I'd been appointed the small-town token spokesperson. It was almost funny; if they only knew. Despite the comedic aspect, I didn't want to talk about race to anyone white, not strangers and I damn sure wasn't ready to talk about it to Cindy.

I purchased X's autobiography and quietly slid it into my bag. A slight secret smile played at the corners of my lips knowing there would be a stowaway passenger on our plane ride home.

Journalist Alex Haley, author of *Roots: The Saga of an American Family*, and coauthor of X's autobiography captivated me from the very first line.

"When my mother was pregnant with me, she told me later, a party of hooded Ku Klux Klan riders galloped up to our home in Omaha, Nebraska, one night." (X, Malcolm, 1998)

The story ends with those same hooded KKK members terrorizing the Little family and burning their home down with three small children nearly dying inside. Each page incited a nearly tangible resentment of white people in me. Haunted by the painful truths of this country, X's searing tales revealed blinders I hadn't realized I was wearing. I had been raised as if I too were white. Reading the perverse and unearned white entitlement sickened me. What was difficult to accept is I "benefited" from that entitlement, a veritable luxury by association. What did all of that say about me? Malcolm X had not lived to know he had incited a war within this biracial girl's mind. However, both sides of my heart were losing.

How do I explain the feeling of never belonging anywhere or to anyone? Not being able to categorize myself. No label to fit into. No identity to claim. When the most concrete aspect of your identity is not having one, you feel lost. The world we live in seeks—no, demands—to classify all things and people. The white identity I had been wearing never fit right, like an ill-fitting dress you spend all day trying to adjust to no avail. Now there's just a void as if the ill-fitting dress didn't get an invitation to this new party.

I had been raised in all-white schools, all-white neighborhoods, and raised to believe that I too was white. No matter that I never felt like I fit in. I didn't understand what it meant to be Black or to have Black experiences. While I felt like an outsider in my own family, I did not know what it meant to be persecuted or marginalized by the world at large. Adding insult, the history I had been taught were lies published in volumes of schoolbooks to reinforce white supremacy.

While his earlier life as a street thug didn't spellbind me, knowing what he was to become compelled me to keep reading. In the beginning, my anger was fueled by the atrocity that befell Malcom's father. He was murdered by cowardly white men in the KKK. (X, Malcolm, 1998)

"We're gonna take you out there and show you what we do to nigger girls!" rings in my head as I read the words on the page.

The cafeteria flashback was less than a year old. My stomach clenched as I remembered that day. Those were only threats. I was able to push past those goons and go home that day. Mr. Little never had that chance. My face burned with anger. My heart ached for the terror he would've experienced in his last moments. Was he mourning all the things he would never get to see his children through? Was he terrified that he wouldn't be there to protect them? Had he said he loved his wife before he left that day?

His life, like countless thousands of lives before him, was cut down needlessly, from fear, from hate, from soulless people. My mouth soured and I let the book drop onto my bed, as if the painful words contained within were contagious. I'd been engrossed in the story for over an hour. Anger simmered inside my heart threatening mutiny. How can human beings commit such atrocities against one another? How was it possible for men, women, and children to be murdered without consequence? Why is mass murder justified and then overlooked, then rewritten as if it never occurred?

How is it that an entire race of white people was convinced that an entire other race of Black people weren't actual human beings? *How is that fucking possible?* Was there no logic left in the world? Tears stung my eyes, hot against my cheeks as if torched by my anger. I began screaming in my head.

"Why? Why does this happen? How does this happen?"

The human brain is approximately 1.7 million years old. It has one defining skillset, to identify danger and critically assess its options for survival. Historically, humans lived in very hostile environments. Harsh weather elements and wildlife that could mean life or death. Determining if the large shadow, distant on the Serengeti horizon, was a sabretooth tiger was a necessity, not a luxury. X's autobiography illustrated that we have been conditioned to fear one another instead and that fear causes humans to declare war on each other.

There is no sanctuary from my own mind. I cannot go back. I cannot return to the "safety" of my ignorance or isolate myself on an island. I now know I am half Black. Knowledge is not only power, but also a responsibility. Here I was living my whole life as a white person. My mom revealing her lie rocked my world to be sure, but knowing the truth about the history of this country is excruciating.

The truth about my ancestors, well, the white ones, had me hating that part of myself. Those white ancestors committed mass murder, rape, and genocide against my other ancestors, the Black ones. The litany of psychotic atrocities perpetuated by white people is staggering. First, the decimation of the indigenous Native Americans, then enslaving and murdering millions of Africans for four hundred years. That same malicious mindset kept the US silent and complicit in Hitler's reign for over a decade. Then add to that the imprisonment of over 120,000 Japanese Americans in internment camps during World War II. The soil of this country is steeped in the blood of one genocide after the other.

The commotion of raw feelings competes for center stage attention. Like when an airplane experiences extreme turbulence, my emotions are violently tossed around and impossible to control. First, I'm free-falling with confusion, then on solid ground with anger, then hurt kicks me in the gut followed by both shame and rage giving me the one-two punch. I do not have the answers. I don't know what to do about any of it. Yet, my parents are white. *They* are the problem. I am *half* the problem. Generations of white guilt weigh down on me and, in the same breath, so does the burden of living while Black. I feel it when it happens. A looming albatross just found perched on my shoulders and for years it will remain.

Before I began reading this book an hour ago, my ignorance, disguised as freedom, comforted me. I have grown older in this short time; no longer do I feel like a naive nineteen-year-old. Anguish tears at the fibers of my heart. I can physically feel pain. A weariness has crept into my soul without the wisdom to know what to do with it. Nor do I have anyone I can talk to about the place I find myself. The intersection between race, identity, and ambiguity.

Over the years, I have listened to the racial slurs, the slights and biases my family has uttered. A typical Italian family, we gather for the holidays, every holiday, any holiday. Growing up, big family dinners were what we did, and we did them regularly, rotating from this uncle or that aunt's house. My mother, as the oldest sibling, often hosted. The conversations around those dinner tables (we could never fit at just one) after all the mechanic talk (there's a long line of auto mechanics and big truck engine mechanics in my family), often centered around politics, economics, and immigration. Living in a state bordering Mexico, immigration was an unavoidable topic.

"Mexicans are coming here illegally and stealing all of the jobs."

"How are the real Americans supposed to feed our families?"

"Damn spics should be shot on site for trespassing."

An undercurrent of fear seemed ever-present in those conversations. A fear of losing status and power to minorities. Us versus them. A scarcity mindset emerged around those dinner tables. What we kids learned listening (and I was always listening) was that you have to get yours before the next guy, cause some *nigger or spic* was gonna take it from you.

A sociocultural phenomenon developed from centuries propagating the belief that white people constitute a superior race and should therefore dominate society. This of course, is at the exclusion and detriment to all nonwhite ethnic groups. The fear among whites evolved as a backlash from a white supremacy belief system. The fear is that the oppressed will one day rise up and seek revenge. Thus, white America grows anxious about the emerging ethnic and racial diversity. White identity, or as close to white as you can get, gives undeniable historical privilege wherever colonization has existed. That is changing though; since 1954, the US Census Bureau has predicted that the United States will become a "majority-minority" country by 2044.

Picking the book back up, I became increasingly enraged as I read. X's autobiography revealed that the insurance company refused to pay on his father's life insurance policy, corruptly stating Mr. Little had committed suicide, an act not covered. When, in fact, the KKK had murdered him, widowing Mrs. Little and leaving eight children fatherless. This murder tragically altered the trajectory of all nine Littles. At the hands of white people, Malcolm and his siblings essentially became orphaned when the state then forced his mother into a mental institution. (*X, Malcolm, 1998*)

> *"I truly believe that if a state social agency ever destroyed a family, it destroyed ours... And ours was not the only case of this kind."*

—MALCOLM X

My anger burned through me like a flame to dry brush. At first, I couldn't finish, the words were too painful, then it fueled my need to read until the end. I wanted to learn everything I could about Malcolm as a man beyond even this book. I wanted to un-educate myself, then reeducate myself with the truth, not the lies I had been fed all my life.

Some of my family members were less than enthusiastic about my new pursuit. My Uncle Frank, the most financially successful of all his siblings and therefore the de facto patriarch, is one such family member. He saw me reading X's book during a family vacation he was hosting and had a complete meltdown.

"He's a thug looking for attention through hate! *He hated white people!* He wanted all white people to *die!* He preached *murder!*" The last word is hurled at me, spittle flying from his mouth.

"He was not!" I raged back.

We were both stunned by my outburst. He was startled into a brief silence. I have *never* yelled at him. I was shaking with fury, but yelling at an adult was never allowed. Never. As kids, you never even dreamed of such an indiscretion. Defiance simply was not tolerated. But I came out of my body in that moment. My uncle's accusations were wrong. His words lit a fuse in me that was inextinguishable. And just like that, the genie could not be stuffed back into the bottle.

The shock passed and he snatched the book from my hands and hurled it over the side of the boat. "I won't have it!" His words struck me like missiles through my heart.

My eyes stung from trying to hold the fiery tears back. My hands sat empty on my lap mourning their loss. I was alone in my grief, again. It had been such a beautiful day on the lake. We had just finished skiing, the lake was fairly quiet now, no other boats in sight as we anchored to eat lunch. My younger cousins looked like human buoys floating in the water around the back of the boat. Their legs through the arm holes of their life vests so they could float sitting up and eat their ham and cheese sandwiches.

My uncle's outburst came out of nowhere. I was sitting quietly on a bow seat soaking up the sun, reading. I hadn't said a word to anyone. I hadn't made some grand declaration that I was converting to Islam or that I was joining the New Black Panther Party, even though that's what my future held. My quietly reading a book incited a fear in my uncle and that fear manifested in his attempt to thwart, what, I do not know. Maybe he feared what I would become. Maybe he feared what me not being white anymore meant.

Malcolm X was the most outspoken and dynamic leader of the Black Revolution. What he was not was a hate preacher. He never actually advocated for violence, he was an advocate for cultural and social reconstruction and ultimately reconciliation of the races.

"By any means necessary" was a battle cry to urge paralyzed Black people and galvanize their movement toward self-determination. Black people's resolve in this country had been beaten down and X's life mission was to wake up a sleeping people. He wanted Black people to examine their obstacles, determine their vision, find their resolve, and explore their options to dissolve their obstacles (X, Malcolm, 1998). I found myself so utterly enthralled, so totally captivated by his words, I knew that I would never be the same again. I also knew that the day was coming when I would need to choose.

CHAPTER 12

Summers in a small river town are uniquely monotonous. Temperatures of 102°F by 6:00 a.m. send you out to the river as early as you can, seeking relief. River life is a predominant part of Lake Havasu living. You either own a boat, lease a boat, or have a family member who has a boat. From boat dealerships to retail accessory shops, all things water-related was the industry that kept the town afloat (pardon the corny pun).

Water skiing is to Lake Havasu City as football is to southern states. Long before we moved to Arizona, I learned to water ski on vacation with my Uncle Frank's family. Living so close to the lake, I retreated to the water often. I learned to slalom ski and even bought my own bright pink and aquamarine ski. Out there before everyone else, the lake felt like my private meditation refuge.

The early morning dawn glimmers off placid water, undisturbed for miles in every direction. Serene and glassy, the depths of the blue-green lake appear bottomless as if peace was a picture. It was my favorite time of day. I didn't love my time living in Lake Havasu, but these moments made up for the sweltering heat, oppressive town mindset, and the constant stares from the residents.

One random August afternoon, I was at work. The lunch rush had just ended and Cindy and I were resting against the back counter. Against the rules, but we were tired, the restaurant had been slammed for three solid hours. Cindy was chatting away, describing yet again, another nature adventure she and her boyfriend, Jason, had been on the previous weekend. Over the months, Cindy had shared many similar tales, mountain hikes in Northern Arizona, ATV rides in the desert washes, dry flat bottoms of canyons, and camping in the tall pine forests of central Arizona.

Cindy described beautiful, lush mountain landscapes at the many camping trips with Jason's family all over the state. Naively, I assumed Arizona was just one giant desert. Jason's older brother, Jeff, was a whiz at fixing anything broken so I heard of the many saves he'd managed. Jason's family were DIYers of the outdoors. *Nature* magazine could've featured the Hardy family for all of their scenic exploits. It had always been a lifestyle for them, Cindy had said. It only slowed slightly when their dad had suddenly passed away a few years earlier. The boys still lived in the family home on the west side of town. Road bikes, ATVs, and camping gear neatly lined the side yard of their ranch-style house. Grandma Hardy headed up the household of four and traveled on the family escapades despite her age.

Cindy chattered on about their planned evening ATV ride out to Chemehuevi Wash Trail. I honestly hadn't been listening, focusing instead on my upcoming move to Los Angeles. I had been accepted as a transfer student to the University of Southern California. Each day, my attention seemed to be more galvanized by my *own* upcoming adventure. I was so excited to be part of USC's family and explore all that the campus life had to offer. T minus four weeks. Every single hour got counted. I couldn't wait to say goodbye to this town. Good riddance Lake Havasu. My mom never should have chosen this backward-ass place.

"Um, hello! Are you even listening to me?" she asked, clearly irritated.

Guilty, I looked up in surprise. "Sorry, no. What were you saying?"

"You are always daydreaming these days. Your nose is either in those books or in the clouds. Other than the lake, have you even ever seen any of this beautiful state you're about to leave?"

Cindy loved her state. This is where we parted ways. Much to her dismay, countless times I had condemned the entire desert region as a hellhole. She'd grown up here, her loyalty was here.

Yet, I couldn't argue her point. I was leaving in just weeks, and was incapable of differentiating a wash from a sand dune. I shook my head. I hadn't traveled anywhere except for my one trip to Tempe, home of Arizona State University. I only did that to appease my mom, who wanted me to stay close to home for college. I wanted to remind her that Arizona was not our "home," but I kept my mouth shut.

Guilty once again, I shook my head no. She wanted to hear me say it out loud.

"No, I haven't seen anything," I admitted.

And suddenly she was speed talking me.

"Well, that's it! You're coming with us tomorrow. Jeff will be there so you can ride with him. Jason usually stores the packed cooler on the back of Jeff's bike but he'll jerry-rig something else." She was talking so fast that I couldn't keep up.

"I'll go by Jason's when I get off and tell him tonight. And he can tell Jeff to pack an extra helmet and supplies." She continued her instructions for me.

"So as soon as the lunch shift is over tomorrow, get your side work done quickly. Bring shorts and change into your swimsuit. We'll go night swimming after the ride. It's gonna be a blast!"

"Sure," I said. Only sure of one thing, I just got fast talked into this. If she heard the hesitancy in my voice, she didn't let it deter her. I had finally relented and Cindy was vindicated.

I raced down highway 95 the next day to meet the trio. I shifted and pulled my work shirt off, then braked, and pulled up my shorts. My latest mastered skill: changing while driving my manual transmission car. Don't judge me, the perpetually late must multitask. Today was no exception. I was late, as usual, and Cindy was a freak about punctuality. If it wasn't for the fact that she'd been trying to convince me for a year to get my nose out of the books, her ass would have probably left me. My mother was right, I'd be late to my own funeral. Sigh.

Chemehuevi Wash had been named for the Chemehuevi tribe, an indigenous people of the Great Basin. Originally a nomadic desert tribe among the greater nation of Paiute people, they were condemned to reservations in the Mohave desert. The reservation system established tracts of land, often the most undesirable land with the harshest living conditions, for Native Americans to live on while white settlers took over their land. The reservations rendered long-term catastrophic and devastating effects for the indigenous people. Here in Arizona, it didn't seem much better than Utah a decade-and-a-half ago. (SCTCA, 2021)

Properly attired, helmet in hand, I stood next to the ATV, slightly out of breath from my sprint to the meet-up spot. I avoided Cindy's glare as I took my place next to Jeff's quad. I knew she'd been compulsively checking her watch like a card-carrying OCD member.

I thanked the weather gods for the warm breeze, it was blazing, and the current lifted the heavy curtain of dark curls off my shoulders. A brief reprieve for the near constant dampness on the back of my neck. For eighteen months, any time spent outside elicited the same suffocating feeling. The temperature gauge in my car had read 112°F. The sunbaked earth felt even hotter than the air—I was certain hell wasn't this damn hot!

"God, I will not miss this damn heat!" I burst out. Out of the air-conditioned car less than three minutes and small beads of sweat had already formed on my forehead and other places I'd rather not describe. I dreaded putting the helmet on, knowing for sure I would suffocate.

"Am I gonna die with this thing on?" Holding up the heavy, red-flamed helmet, I inquired with all the dramatic flair I could muster. In my defense, this heat did feel like a form of death. Plus, the irony of the hell imagery on the helmet was not lost on me. Eighteen months of what felt like purgatory, was long enough. I learned I would never ever live in the desert again.

Jeff looked up from strapping the cooler packed with ice, cold beers, and two wine coolers for me (I hate beer) to the storage rack. It was the first time I had seen more than the back of his head. He had dirty blonde hair and the sun was teasing out streaks of strawberry reds. He had the brightest blue eyes I had ever seen. The blue was so brilliant and clear, the saying *I could get lost in your eyes* flashed in my mind. He stood about six feet tall, fit but with a slight beer belly.

Rolling his brilliant blues but laughing at my antics, Jeff responded with a confident, "Of course not. You're in good hands."

Oh, he clearly did not know the length my theatrics traveled. Was he referring to the heat or reassuring me that I wouldn't die while riding with him? I had questions, but decided that five minutes after meeting someone was too soon to reveal my very real paranoia of death by hot air. I'd ridden ATVs before; I'd even learned to drive them in middle school, but I hadn't been on one since. We started out slow. Maybe my viselike death grip around Jeff's waist influenced his initial snail-paced speed. Reactively clutching him tighter at every bump and gear shift, breathing couldn't have been easy for him. I didn't care, I was trying not to die.

Suddenly, Jason yelled out, "Let's *go!*"

He and Cindy were way ahead and impatient with our slow progress. Grateful that the helmet hid my panicked expression, I gripped tighter, and Jeff opened up the throttle. Jeff was a skilled driver and his ATV mastery quickly became obvious. I relaxed just a bit.

Turns out whizzing through the wash around countless desert bushes and cacti was exhilarating. We raced Jason and Cindy for miles and miles of twists and turns. Jeff skillfully avoided eating their dust cloud as we topped out at forty miles an hour. My heart raced, and I laughed at every unexpected jolt. Jeff pinned the throttle, and we'd launch to the left or right just in the nick of time, missing some random desert plant life.

"*Braaaap!*" the bikes echoed throughout the long valley. The quad's rugged tire thread ate up the hardened sandy ground. I whooped and hollered; I couldn't believe how much fun I was having. After what felt like hours, we coasted onto a sandy beach on the Southern Coast of the lake. The dark-green water was lapping the sandy edges. The sun was setting over the lake.

Admittedly, the most beautiful sunsets I had ever experienced were here in the desert. Mid-dismount from the quad, Jeff and I paused simultaneously and wordlessly lowered ourselves back into our seats. The sun was retiring behind the mountains and the palette of colors lit up the entire sky. For nearly ten minutes we stared in awe. The absence of bright city lights and manufactured smog freed God's imagination. The cloudless sky flashed fevered reds and fuchsia pinks so painfully beautiful it nearly hurt staring at the display. It felt like we could see God from there. I had no idea that was the moment that would change everything.

We were at the southern side of the lake. Any houses were miles away. We had the beach to ourselves. We sprawled out, cooler propped open between the four of us, sipping from our cans. Cindy and I fell into our normal habit of restaurant gossip, speculating which server was sleeping with which celebrity customer.

"So, what did you think of your first desert ATV ride?" Jeff interjected into our conversation.

I was about to give him some flippant sarcastic remark about my near-death experience, but the earnest look on his face changed my mind. He genuinely wanted to know. Was that also a bit of nervousness I detected in his voice?

"Actually, I had a blast. I was a little nervous at first."

"A little?" interrupted Jeff with a huge smirk on his face.

"Yes, a little," I said with all the defiance of a four-year-old.

We both laughed. The stars began their dazzling parade across the blackened sky. Inspiration hitting me, I jumped up and peeled my shorts and shirt off. My bathing suit stuck to my damp skin, gritty from sweat and dust. The water promised relief. I tossed my shirt in Jeff's direction and raced for the water. The cool water beckoned.

"Race you!" I called over my shoulder.

Jeff hesitated, looking out into the darkness, then relented when I called him a "scaredy cat."

Jason said he had to be up early for work. He and Cindy headed back, calling over the loud ATV they'd see us tomorrow. Jeff and I waved goodbye then ran for the water. We laughed and splashed each other like seven-year-olds. I dove in and relished the coolness the water offered. Jeff followed suit and we swam for a while. Standing in shallow waters, Jeff snuck up behind me and dunked me. I recovered quickly and attempted my own sneak attack; instead, everything changed in an instant. Suddenly Jeff was kissing me.

Mr. Finn was droning on about simplifying fractions, but I was barely listening. The first spring flowers were blooming outside, and they had stolen my attention. It was last period on a Friday afternoon, and I was just looking forward to walking home with Carrie Miller. She was my new friend, my only friend, actually. Montevideo was my fifth elementary school and although I've been here since September, I didn't have any friends yet. Well, that was not until this morning.

Ms. Brisk, the kindergarten teacher, randomly stopped Carrie and me this morning. We were both dropping our younger brothers off in the lower grade hall. I had seen her there many mornings, and even though we were in the same class, she had never spoken to me. I'm not surprised. It's always the same. I'm the new kid with the strange hair who didn't look like anyone else. Friend-making has never been a skillset I mastered.

"Excuse me ladies," Ms. Brisk interrupted our walk back down the hall.

"I noticed you both are on this hall every morning before—"

"Stop running in the halls, Michael and Brian!" she yelled, interrupting herself as two boys leading four other second-grade boys raced down the hall, crashing into each other as they did. We both looked up surprised, trying to avoid getting hit by their flailing backpacks. The brightly colored hall separating the classrooms was wide and noisy from the laughs and squeals of dozens of excited little voices.

"As I was saying—"

"Ms. Brisk! Ms. Brisk!" yelled a young, blonde, pigtailed girl.

Ms. Brisk rolled her eyes, looked directly at the young girl sternly and said to Carrie and me: "As you can see, my hands are full here trying to wrangle the unruly. Would you two be willing to come each morning to help supervise the kids before class begins?"

"Yes, of course!" Carrie and I said in unison, then looked at each other and smiled.

"Great! I will see you both Monday morning at 7:45," Ms. Brisk said while grabbing yet another boy attempting to chase the class hamster. He was clutching the empty cage trying to defend himself.

"How was I supposed to know he was gonna run out if I opened the door?"

That was all it took. Carrie and I talked the whole way back to our hall. She was the oldest of four kids. She and her family had lived in Mission Viejo her whole life. She loved math and hated Lincoln Logs, because her brothers never cleaned up and she had stepped barefooted on her fair share. *Little House on the Prairie* was her favorite show, but she also had to endure watching *The Dukes of Hazzard* since it was her brother's favorite.

At 3:05 p.m., the bell rang, and Carrie waited for me near the end of the building. On our walk home, Carrie chatted tirelessly about John Calvin, the *famous* John Calvin. Famous in our sixth-grade class, that is. John was taller than all the other boys with dark hair, green eyes, and a thousand-watt smile. He reminded me of what my uncles must've looked like at his age. All the girls loved him. For his part, John did his best to spread his attention around to all of his fans. I hadn't noticed boys much before, not in that way. However, John was my assigned desk mate and just by close proximity, I started paying attention too. Although we sat six inches apart, he never said one word to me. Eventually, I too joined the John Infatuation Fan Club. For his part, John never even noticed me. I shouldn't have been surprised. Not one time had any boy ever liked me. I was the different girl.

"You're dirty!" echoed in my head and reminded me why.

I didn't know then that it would be another two years before a boy would notice me, and that boy wouldn't look anything like John Calvin.

Two years later, we still lived in Mission Viejo and there was no indication a move was on the horizon, which surprised everyone. Although my mom was not in the military, we moved like she was. Historically, Sandy gets an idea and suddenly a realtor is hammering in a For Sale sign in our front yard. Mission Viejo was the nicest town we had lived in yet. Its upper-middle-class neighborhoods displayed all the accoutrements of up-and-coming suburbanites, including its own private manmade lake and country club. What it did share with all our other former neighborhoods was that it was lily-white. Everyone looked the same: all white.

One summer day, when I was thirteen, our doorbell rang. I was the only one home, so the shock was only mine when I opened our front door. Standing on our porch was the darkest-skinned teenage boy I had ever seen holding a duffle bag stuffed with various small toys. Immediately, I was fascinated. Where did he come from? I literally stepped out onto the porch looking past him for what, I do not know. Maybe an answer to why I had never seen him before. If he lived here, I would've definitely noticed him. He didn't look like anyone in this community. His flawless ebony skin was beautiful to me. My stomach immediately started to flutter, and I stammered when I opened my mouth to speak. I had never felt any of these feelings before. Not even for John Calvin—and never for a boy that looked like this young man.

His name was Dee, short for De'leon. Dee explained that his school football team was fundraising for the upcoming season. He lived and went to school twenty minutes away. His team coach had driven all the players to the "nice" neighborhood to door knock selling snacks and small toys for donations. Dee said they would be coming every day that week. He was supposed to go to different streets each day. Instead, he came back to my house every day. I looked forward to seeing him each afternoon. We sat on the porch and talked the whole time he was there. I used my whole savings from my allowance to buy the entire contents of his bag just so he wouldn't get in trouble. On the last day, he asked me to be his girlfriend. My face flushed and the butterflies were back. Up until then, I was the only one home when he came. My parents were both working, so they didn't even know Dee existed. I said yes but had no idea how I was going to tell my parents I had a Black boyfriend.

———

Jeff and I stayed in that lake intermittently laughing, splashing, and kissing until well past midnight. I had no idea this was even possible. I was nineteen. No white boy, no white man, no white anyone had ever found me attractive. Yet here I was, standing with this man, listening to him tell me how utterly beautiful I was. What I was, was profoundly astonished.

Thoughts of watching the disappointed look on my mom's face when I told her about Dee flashed in my mind.

"Are you sure this is a good idea?" she had asked, reducing Dee down to a *"this."*

As if I had disobeyed an unwritten rule, I apologized. For what, I did not know. What I did know, was that I didn't want to disappoint my mom. Why couldn't she understand that none of the boys in our neighborhoods ever liked me? Now, would she finally be proud? Would my choice in boyfriends finally earn her approval?

It was too dark for Jeff to see the tears in my eyes.

CHAPTER 13

"Ain't nothing changed but the year it is."

—ANONYMOUS

The history of this country's abuse and terrorism of people of color is undeniable.

The year of 1492 marked the beginning of centuries of transatlantic colonization when the land was systematically stolen from an entire race of indigenous people, falsely named Indians. The reward for welcoming the fair-skinned seamen was decimation. The history was then rewritten and every documentation of the retelling celebrated Europeans. They were not accurately named as the murderers, rapists, thieves, and pillagers their actions demonstrated. Then, for over four hundred years, the stolen land was massively developed with shackled blood, sweat, and tears of tens of millions of enslaved Africans. The reign of terror continued even after the Emancipation Proclamation freed the enslaved people. Jim Crow laws were quickly established as a legal system of racial segregation to marginalize African Americans. The menacing laws denied them the right to vote, hold jobs, get an education, seek proper housing, and many other opportunities. Simultaneously, white supremacy mindset gave rise to the hate group Ku Klux Klan. For decades thereafter, African Americans were hunted and murdered legally and publicly. This tyrannical oppression continued for another one hundred long years, birthing impoverished slums in every major city condemning Black Americans to severe and generational poverty. (Alexander, 2020)

The oppressors, wrapped in the cloak of patriotism and religious superiority, believed they were entitled to oppress. They believed they were superior. That mindset has never changed. The oppression never ended. I would argue that the past never was the past, only a continuation of the same brutal terrorism. At some point, the oppressed will always find a way to rise up.

March 1991 found South Central Los Angeles a cauldron of simmering long-standing racial tensions. The unemployment rate was about 50 percent, a drug epidemic was ravaging the area, gang activity and violent crimes were the tragic consequences. Continuing unanswered desperate frustrations about abhorrent living conditions and long-standing tension between police and residents over the years were explosive factors igniting the Los Angeles uprising. On March 3, 1991, Los Angeles resident Rodney King was savagely beaten for a reported fifteen minutes by four white Los Angeles Police Department officers. The video captured by a bystander, released days after the incident, showed King being kicked repeatedly, being beaten with batons while more than a dozen cops stood by watching and commenting on the beating. Ultimately, the four officers were only charged with excessive use of force. A year later, on April 29, 1992, a jury consisting of twelve residents from the distant suburbs of Ventura County (nine white, one Latino, one biracial, one Asian) found the four officers not guilty. (Alexander, 2020)

Further fueling the outrage was the tragic murder of a fifteen-year-old African American girl named Latasha Harlins. Thirteen days after the brutal beating and hospitalization of Rodney King, Latasha Harlins was murdered by a Korean liquor store owner. He shot her in the back of her head because he believed she was trying to steal a one dollar and seventy-nine cents bottle of orange juice. She was found clutching two dollars in her hand. Although the maximum sentence for his crime was sixteen years, the store owner received probation and a $500 fine. (Feder-Haugabook, 2021)

The 1992 Los Angeles riots following the Rodney King beating trial led to the deaths of sixty-three people and were a grim reminder that you can only keep your foot on the neck of the oppressed for so long. Pressure will rise and the human instinct for survival will prevail. Retribution does not just injure the guilty, however.

In the wake of those burning buildings, the stench of smoldering poverty, injustice, and brutality hovered over the city, a veritable malignant cancer. Just a few months later, on the heels of the uprising, racial tensions still palpable, I stepped onto the University of Southern California's campus as a transfer student.

August heat in Los Angeles was a relief at only 91°F. It had been a sweltering 119°F when we left Lake Havasu at dawn that morning. The manicured ivy-covered red brick buildings and towering arches are just the beginning of the beauty of this campus. University of Southern

California's parklike grounds cover 229 acres in the middle of South Central Los Angeles. Within the walls of the campus, there's a vibrant mix of green and park spaces, fountains and sculptures, and contemporary and traditional architecture. There are endless brick pathways that travel between theaters and lecture hall buildings. The massive, ornately-carved arches greet you at every building entrance. I felt like an intellectual of old here, a genuine *Dead Poets Society* experience. I loved everything about this campus.

I welcomed the summer breeze dancing through my curls as I followed the signs directing us to Birnkrant Residential College, my new dorm building. After we unloaded, my parents kissed me goodbye and made their last trip down the three flights of stairs; the elevator had been jammed for over an hour with all the new move-ins. Instead of the euphoria I was certain I was going to feel, terror was settling in like cold, wet blankets lain over horses to cool down their overheated bodies. I'm nineteen-and-a-half for goodness sake, I tell myself. I am an adult and yet the same nervous feeling of being the new kid in class emerges. I am standing inside the side entrance of Birnkrant hall, my key card hasn't been working, so I don't dare walk them outside to their car for fear of getting locked out. There is this sense of abandonment rising in my throat watching my parents buckle into their seats.

I don't know where this feeling is coming from. Hadn't I wanted to be a Trojan? Hadn't I begged my mom to allow me to apply when we visited for a campus tour? Hadn't I then paid the application fee? Then spent hours on my application, typing it on my new Brother Electric GX-750

Correctronic typewriter. Not trusting the college computer lab, too afraid it would randomly delete my work again. Then I begged my English professor to grade my application writing sample. Hadn't I poured my soul into writing the entrance writing essay on what *The Autobiography of Malcolm X* meant to me? Hadn't he given me an A? Hadn't the professor said I would be a great addition to USC, that they would be glad to have me?

So why was I standing there feeling like I didn't belong? Like I didn't have what it took to survive here. Sweat trickled down the back of my neck.

I was standing behind my seat in third grade. I couldn't sit because there was a pile of baby diapers stacked neatly on my desk chair. The day before was the first day of school. I wore my favorite bright yellow terrycloth dress with the matching belt. I wanted desperately for this school to be different. It was my third elementary school. My mom didn't like the new house, so I wasn't very hopeful that we'd be here very long, but I kept my fingers crossed anyway. All I wanted was to make friends, to just fit in. Just once.

The morning had been long with the teacher taking extra time to orient the students to her classroom rules and expectations. She wasn't taking any questions, so no matter how many times I raised my hand, she ignored me. I had drunk two large glasses of orange juice that morning at breakfast. It had been a special treat from my dad. I think he was trying to help me feel less nervous. I had repeated his encouraging words on my walk to school. I wasn't familiar with the new school, so I was late finding my classroom. My new teacher was not pleased when I finally strolled in seven minutes late.

So when she wouldn't acknowledge my hand, I didn't know what to do. I had to pee so badly. Panic started to flood my veins because I didn't even know where the bathrooms were. So I continued to sit, legs crossed willing my bladder to cooperate, hand silently raised. Finally, my ten-year-old bladder was forced to surrender its contents and I felt hopeless when, under my seat, a large yellow puddle formed.

As the other students became aware of what had happened, they all began to yell as if they were in imminent danger and the pee was going to jump on them. For my part, I sat paralyzed. I was frozen in a mix of shame and the worst kind of *"please dear God let me die"* embarrassment. I had never endured such public disgrace. Hot tears stung my eyes and refused to stay in place. Exacerbating my humiliation, the tears stung my burning cheeks. I couldn't look up. I began willing myself to disappear. I refused to lift my head, refused to meet anyone's judgment. I cried for all the possibilities lost, for the friends who I would never have. For the slumber parties I wouldn't receive invitations to, for all the lunches I would spend sitting alone.

In mid-sentence and with high annoyance, the teacher exclaimed, "What on Earth is going o—?" her question trailed off as she walked toward my desk and answered her own question. "Recess!" she yelled. "Ms. Yardley, take everyone to the playground. *Now!*"

As the kids filed out, I heard them snickering. Out of the corner of my eye I caught them pointing their little niggling, self-righteous fingers at me.

I shouldn't have been surprised by the diapers. Some little snot probably stole them from their baby brother or sister's diaper bag. It was cruel, but I knew the taunts were coming. I begged my mom to let me stay home. I told her I had polio. It was the only really bad disease I knew of. I couldn't bear the thought of telling her what actually happened. How was I supposed to know that it had been eradicated?

I was a latchkey kid; I wore our house key on a chain around my neck. After the incident yesterday, my teacher had sent me home. I begged her not to call my mom to pick me up. Apparently, she had a heart after all. I walked home from school, in my pretty yellow dress wet with urine and let myself into an empty house. So no one was ever the wiser that I had come home, changed, and washed my clothes.

The taunting went on for over a month until a better news cycle came along. During a morning recess, Tommy Knudson, standing on top of the jungle gym, was showing off his latest Tarzan moves by pounding his chest. He fell from the top bar striking his face on another bar on his way down. He knocked out his two front teeth and blackened his left eye. I never liked Tommy because he was the taunting ringleader; but that day I was grateful for him. Also, to the man upstairs because I was no longer newsworthy.

———

Standing inside the glass door of the residence hall long after my parents had driven away, I felt utterly alone. The feeling was so unexpected. Like the vast aloneness I felt all those nights lying flat on my back on our still warm sunbaked driveway in Arizona. I'd watch the millions of stars so brilliantly lit that only a sky void of city lights can debut.

I had set all of this in motion. USC's application process was seven months and I pursued it doggedly without cease. I celebrated each small victory. I planned, studied at community college, saved my money, and visualized myself as a Trojan. Even when the acceptance letter came, my mom and I danced together celebrating my triumph.

"Is this what you truly want?" she had asked me.

"Of course, Mom!" I exclaimed with all the confidence of a naive nineteen-year-old.

Was there a doubt then? Did I question my ability? *No*! So why now? Why am I always so afraid?

CHAPTER 14

It doesn't take long for the newness of university life to begin to dim; in its place is a rising disturbance in my gut. In the same way a deadly ocean undercurrent is undetectable above the surface, I too feel an insatiable angry undercurrent. There is a reason USC has the nickname University of Spoiled Children; there is a tremendous amount of wealth walking around these grounds.

At first, I was mesmerized with campus life and living on such a rich and elite campus. I felt like I had been transported out of Los Angeles. Out of South Central. Out of drive-through windows equipped with bulletproof slide-out boxes that prevent any direct human contact. Out of drug central parkway intersecting with gang banging boulevard. Out of a dirty, unsafe, dangerous, "lock your doors the moment you get in your car" city.

The university is a closed campus, protected by sturdy red brick walls, guarded by manned gated entrances. Ensuring its longevity, USC appeased parents of trust fund babies turned college students and generous charitable donors alike. Those walls engender safety, an intentionally manufactured freedom created by the founders for the privileged intellectual community that resides within.

The immaculate ivy-covered, brick buildings stand powerful and majestic. There is an other-worldliness feel to them. There are no crumbling housing projects; no homeless men, women, or children; no soliciting prostitutes; and no suspicious men trading narcotics for cash. Growing up, we moved a lot yes, but always within the suburbs of Orange County, an hour from the city. I don't possess city swag, the cool aloofness that long-term exposure stark poverty is bred from. I am essentially ill-equipped for life on the outside of the university walls. Yet, I relish life on the inside.

On campus, the miniature green rolling hill area between the music hall and music theater was my favorite outdoor place to study. Every day, including weekends, practicing music students position themselves to capture the best acoustics. Rousing sounds of classical music I'd never heard before and deep melodic rhythms of jazz reverberated off of the nearby buildings filling me with a great sense of hope. Sitting there alone those afternoons, I was so grateful for my ears. Blissfully listening as I studied one subject after the next, realizing I may be alone, but I was never lonely. It was there in that spot the anger was re-triggered.

Only a year ago, reading Malcom X's autobiography ignited a tumultuous churning in my spirit. As if being on this campus, living so carefree in the wake of the Rodney King beating and all of the atrocities of the past were catching up. As if they were weighing down on me, calling me into action. I collided directly into the restlessness, literally. I was rounding a corner to one of the buildings when I bumped into Nicole Wilson. Nikki, to all her friends, was the resident advisor who hosted me and another girl during our Weekend on Campus event eight months ago.

Nikki was kind and wise and Black. She was my age yet nearly two years ahead of me in school. I, a would-be transfer student, had to take multiple remediation courses to be ready to apply to college. This compared to Nikki, who entered USC as a freshman and former high school valedictorian. The weekend event was designed to entice potential students by giving them a taste of what student life would look like at USC. Nikki had impressed me the moment she spied me standing alone after all of my fellow potentials had been paired up. Somehow, my name had fallen through the cracks and I was unassigned. The university gave me the greatest blessing by forgetting me.

"Come on girl! Us Black folks gotta stick together!" were her very first words to me. I loved her instantly.

We spent the weekend together, her "schooling" me on everything black at USC. The dos, the don'ts, and how to get the most out of being a Trojan. The *Five Heartbeats* movie was showing at the Ray Stark Family Theater and Nikki added it to our night agenda. It felt like divine timing. We talked until nearly dawn the next morning discussing the story of the rise and fall of an African American singing group. Nikki offered her perspective on the potentially dangerous pitfalls awaiting Black performers without proper representation. I left that weekend experience certain of two things, Nikki and I would be friends forever and the only college mascot I would ever claim was a Trojan.

This was the pre-cellphone, pre-Facebook era, so when I finally arrived on campus six months later, I didn't know how to find Nikki. Making matters worse, I didn't remember her last name. So, when I collided into her outside of Annenberg School of Communication, it was fate. Per my usual, I was lost and late again; I literally dropped what I was carrying to hug her. To my delight, she remembered me and hugged me back. I hadn't made any friends yet and was so relieved to find her. Another point for fate's team.

Nikki and I became inseparable after our reuniting. It was her senior year and she was in her prime. It felt like she ruled that campus. Everywhere we went, people, professors, and students alike, greeted her warmly with genuine joy to see her. Nikki had a one thousand-watt smile she generously shared. She was the president of the Black Student Assembly, an umbrella student-led organization that governed all the Black student organizations on campus. I enjoyed watching her skillfully conduct the meetings, managing differing and often contrary personalities, each vying for center stage. She had a low melodic speaking voice, and I admired her patience and ability to make everyone feel heard and appreciated. After all, these student leaders gathered each week to unify under one banner and goal: committed to improving the Black student experience at a predominantly white institution.

My declared major was political science. The life of an attorney had been alluring to me for close to two years. Trial dates, closing arguments, being on the right side of the law, and serving justice beckoned. Never mind that Kevin Costner had just come alive on the big screen as the District Attorney in the smash hit movie *JFK*. I wanted more than anything to stand in a courtroom as did he and sanctimoniously deliver the facts of an uncovered conspiracy.

I was driven by another force, though. I yearned to learn the true African American history. Not the lies I had been told all my life. My mission was clear, I was to declare it as my minor. Therein lay my problem. The university didn't actually have African American anything as a field of study students could declare. According to USC's board of academic scholars, there were no ethnic majors at all. Undaunted by the university's lack of diverse majors, I doubled down on my personal studies. Increasingly, I became more committed to righting the wrongs done to Black people in this country.

Bookstores were my favorite hangout; I'd spend hours reading (for free). I quickly learned that bookstores allowed you to peruse their shelves at your leisure and even provided comfy chairs to sample their products. Books like the *Iceman Inheritance* rocked my world. Author Michael Bradley argues that racism, the threat of nuclear war, environmental pollution, and other social problems are the result of the behavior, values, and psychology of the white race. This was so revelatory to me, eighteen years of being white and never once had I ever heard a white person admit being white was problematic. Bradley presented evidence that there was actual science to white entitlement and I was enthralled.

Increasingly, I became frustrated with what was being taught in my actual classes. The lack of any acknowledgment of African contributions to the arts and sciences was infuriating. A continuation of my primary and secondary education perpetrating lies that human history began in Europe. Yet the evidence was irrefutable. Museums around the globe housed artifacts confirming the continent of Africa as the birthplace of both basic and advanced mathematics, science, and written communication.

Thousands of years ago, Africans were using numerals, algebra, and geometry in daily life. This knowledge began to spread throughout the world through a series of migrations out of Africa beginning around 30,000 BC. Swaziland is the discovery place of the oldest measuring device, the Lebombo bone, dating back to 35,000 BC. The Democratic Republic of Congo produced the world's oldest evidence of advanced mathematics, the Ishango bone, dating back to 20,000 BC. (Van Sertima, 1983)

The world's oldest examples of geometry and algebra are depicted on papyrus excavated from Kemet's thirteenth dynasty, dating back to 2000 BC. Southern Egypt is the discovery site of yet more papyrus recordings. There are twenty plus pages of advanced arithmetics, calculating the volume of rectangular and cylindrical granaries with pi. (Blatch, 2013)

Ancient Africa is also the birthplace of ancient writing systems and is home to the first identifiable proto-writing, one-hundred-thousand-year-old engravings uncovered in the Blombos Cave in South Africa. Africa's advanced writing system is over six thousand years old, contrasted with Europe's oldest writing, Greek, which has only been in use since 1400 BC. In addition, the Greek language was largely derived from an older African script called proto-Sinaitic.

Timbuktu in Mali is home to the world's oldest university system, Sankore. This was where advanced learning had been taking place for thousands of years. As many as seven hundred thousand scripts have been rediscovered, attesting to the knowledge and practice of advanced mathematics and sciences. West African cities like Gao, Kan, and Timbuktu were literary centers full of libraries with mathematics, astronomy, religious, poetic, legal, and administrative writing systems. (Woods, 1988)

I learned in my studies outside the classroom that long before European colonization, Africa was a thriving continent. By their own admission in history books, Europeans, and later white Americans, have an enormous capacity for the perpetration of physical violence against other cultures. Ancient European culture and behavior depicted in their own books described the insanity. American history alone demonstrates white people's complete lack of regard for human life resulting in antihuman and genocidal terrorism of people of color.

On what was otherwise a beautiful spring day, I sat on my favorite hill between the music hall and the music theater choking on my anger. Nearby, a student played soft murmurs of a jazz scale, the breeze slightly ruffling the pages of the book I held. I had been reading about the Tulsa Race Massacre, a barbaric atrocity committed in 1921. As a violent chill shot down my spine, I shuddered and began to shiver despite the 82°F weather. An internal inferno had been sparked and a raging new anger emerged. An anger that would take years of therapy to reconcile.

Black Wall Street, as it was known, was a miniature version of a modern metropolis, located in the Greenwood District of Tulsa, Oklahoma. Black Wall Street was one of the most affluent thriving communities in the US. It boasted an independent school system, a bank, a hospital, two theaters, and a public transit system. Media was also an integral part of Greenwood. Of the two newspapers, the *Tulsa Star* became Greenwood's primary news source, providing information about legal rights and current events that could affect African Americans. (Tulsa, 2021)

Segregation, Jim Crow laws, and a white intolerance for the existence of freed Black people coalesced into the worst act of American terrorism and racism in American history. White Tulsa's business elite resented the competition that Black Wall Street represented. They could not tolerate that the face of their competition was Black.

June 1, 1921, marked the date of the Tulsa Race Massacre. White residents turned vigilantes, murdered Black residents of the Greenwood District at will. They committed the bloodiest, barbaric atrocities and then looted and burned down the community. More than 1,400 homes, a dozen churches, five hotels, thirty-one restaurants, four drugstores, and eight doctors' offices, as well as a public library and a hospital were burned. These terrorists' acts left nearly ten thousand Black people homeless. Most savagely though, three hundred Black residents were murdered that night and nearly one thousand more were treated for serious injuries. What I haven't said yet was that this horrific massacre was incited because a Black man, Dick Rowland, simply rode in an elevator with a white woman. (Tulsa, 2021)

From that moment on, I was infinitely changed. Knowing about that gruesome, heinous massacre forever tainted my view of white people. It was what tipped the scales for me. I would never again entrust my safety or well-being to white folks. I became hellbent on becoming as Black as I could be. I would not show up in the world as a biracial woman. *I* was a *Black* woman. The way I saw it, I had eighteen years to compensate for. Eighteen years that had been stolen from me.

I twisted up my curls in big Janet Jackson braids (think *Poetic Justice*). I pierced my nose with a big gold ring. I joined the New Black Panther Party. I wanted to remove the façade of the great white man and expose the inner workings of the global white supremacy agenda. I wore T-shirts that read *"Socrates was a Thief," "Hippocrates was a Plagiarist,"* and *"Christopher Columbus was a Murderer."* I could often be heard saying things like "Down with whitie!" "Black Power!" "Liberate your minds brothers and sisters!"

I only hung out with Black students and the more I studied, the more my mistrust of white people deepened. I started saying things like "Damn white folks" or "Ain't that just like white folks."

To counter the demonism of white colonialism, I also read about the ancient Egyptians and the African dynasties of Kings and Queens. I became empowered with the knowledge that Black people, my people, did not come from slaves and were truly the first humans, i.e., Lucy, the oldest human remains that were discovered in 1974 in Ethiopia. (Blatch, 2013)

I felt like Malcom X when he was incarcerated. My miseducation, my hidden heritage, now fully revealed, forever changed the trajectory of my life and it was never going to be the same again. I was becoming a Black nationalist, advocating for unity and political self-determination for Black people, and I was in full support of a separate Black nation.

How in the hell, you might be wondering, was my family receiving the "new" me? Not well, I'm afraid. And for my part, I was not easing them into my transition. Instead, I was pouring gallon after gallon of gasoline on a fire that was destined to leave some casualties.

The LA riots and their accompanying fires were not that far in the rearview mirror. I knew my actions were creating their own inferno. One day, I overheard my mother tell her sister that I had "gone to hell." I knew she was referring to the city that had been burned up. But I also assumed she meant my refusal to stay "white." She did not, could not, understand my metamorphosis. Hell, I didn't understand what was happening. I barely understood that my cocooning caterpillar was emerging as an entirely different species. I left for USC dating a white guy. Yet, everything I had ever known would never be the same again. In those moments, I knew that I could never marry a white man. My worlds were colliding. A veritable personal galaxy supernova. Overcompensating for all that I had perceived I had missed out on; I took a giant leap off of a cliff and became Super Black.

I had no idea then that my metamorphosis would take on a leadership role. In twelve short months from then, the campus would be plastered with signs reading "VOTE FOR BARB!"

CHAPTER 15

I could no longer ignore the obvious. While I believe that I loved Jeff, I refused to raise biracial children. I refused to recreate my life. I refused to burden children with having to choose race or, worse, have the world choose for them. The history between the races is too volatile, too painfully tragic, and here I was trying to carve out my own *very* Black life. Mostly, I could not ignore my growing distrust of white people.

It was supposed to be a short weekend road trip to Phoenix. Just a fun getaway. We would stay with his sister, Jen, and her husband. I hadn't been to Phoenix in a long time. "It would be fun," Jeff said. "I'd enjoy it," he said.

I wasn't particularly close to Jeff's sister. Okay, fine, we weren't friends at *all*. Not since the first day we met. The issue happened at that first meeting. I mean, how was I supposed to know she wasn't pregnant? I thought I was being thoughtful. As I stepped into the small rowboat (the four of us were going fishing), I excitedly exclaimed my congratulations on her pregnancy. Then inserted the rest of my foot in my mouth and asked when she was due. Her belly was significantly distended. Juxtapose that against her rather thin legs and I was 1,000 percent certain she was expecting. I was agonizingly, painfully, and thoroughly wrong. She was not then, nor ever had been, pregnant.

Side note: I have never since then, never one time, asked another woman about her pregnancy, no matter how obvious it is. Unless I hear directly from a woman's own mouth *"I am pregnant,"* my lips are sealed. Even if birth is eminent, I still ain't saying a word without confirmation!

That day on the lake was the longest day of my life. We, Jen and I, sat literally a foot apart, facing each other, no less. The cooler, packed with ice cold drinks sat positioned between her feet. My mouth was parched dry from hours spent in over one-hundred-degree heat, but her ice-cold disdain kept me silent. For her part, Jen generated her own heat-seeking missiles, targeted at my forehead, I imagined. She didn't know Sandy though; I had years of experience in avoiding laser beam glares.

Needless to say, I never did become Jen's favorite person. She sort of just tolerated me, or so I thought. She loved her brothers and the whole family gathered often to fish, camp, and off-road ride. You name it, they did it as a family. Jeff always hoped she and I would become close. I didn't know how to tell him that was never going to happen. Where Jeff was open-minded and uber empathetic, his sister by contrast, was stubborn and overly opinionated (if you asked me), a thought I kept to myself.

This particular weekend was just meant as a getaway for Jeff and I. Our lack of finances meant we needed to stay with Jen and her husband. Jeff and I had spent a delightful afternoon exploring all Phoenix had to offer. It was early evening, around seven o'clock, when we arrived at their apartment. Jen and her husband were taking us to some new swanky restaurant. In the morning, Jeff and I had planned on going to some truck show (I was totally only going for him), and then we'd head back to Havasu afterward. Classes were cancelled that Monday, so I could take my time making the long drive back to USC.

In the bathroom, I could hear raised voices. Jeff was angry. This was odd to me because he had been so happy when we walked in. I opened the door and the voices got louder. Coming down the hall, I heard Jen's husband attempting to keep the peace. His hand was on Jen's shoulder but she was trying to push it away.

Jen kept repeating "Why, Jeff? Why?"

It was more an accusation than a question. Jen was attempting to get in Jeff's face while her husband stepped in between them trying valiantly to prevent it.

Jeff was so angry that his face was almost crimson. As I walked into the living room, everyone went quiet. Jeff did an about-face to shield me from what, I didn't know yet.

He announced, "We're leaving." His voice sounded eerily calm but it didn't match his body language.

My mouth reacted before my thoughts could catch up. "Why on Earth would we do that? We just walked in."

"Funny, *why* is my question too. Isn't it *Jeff*?" Jen prodded.

"Shut the fuck up Jen!" Jeff snarled and I shuddered. The pure anger in his face, I had never seen him like this. He was shaking in fury. A fury I couldn't figure out. Nothing was making sense. I was out of the room for three minutes. Jen started yelling at Jeff again, hurling accusatory questions at him. I didn't actually catch her words because Jeff was now yelling at me.

"We are leaving! Barbara, get your things!"

I hate yelling. The sounds instantly flash to the screams my mother would make from another one of Jim's rampages. Family disputes unnerve me. My mind does this weird thing where everything slows down into slow motion and my body feels like it's standing in molasses. I can't quite get my legs to move but my hands quickly cover my ears.

Instantly, I am four years old again, and the dining room is exploding with broken glass and screams. Food-laden dinner dishes that were once sitting benignly on the table lay crashed on the floor, their former contents slowly sliding down the opposite wall. Jim was screaming that the food was cold, my mom was trying to say that it was hot when she first called him from the barn.

"*Why does she have to argue?*" was my only thought. Then it happened, more plates crash as he leapt to his feet, upsetting the table and everything on it, arms swinging, aiming for her.

"Get your things now!" Jeff was yelling. He was grabbing my arm to pull me into the guest room where our bags were. But he wasn't fast enough, I heard it. I heard her say it and everything goes still. I felt the numbness enveloping my legs.

"*Why* are you with a *nigger*?" The venom in Jen's voice seemed to transform her features. Her pupils constrict and the blue flashes bright like pulling the cord on a neon sign.

My body froze mid step and I turned to look at Jeff, my face contorted in pain. Confused. My mouth no longer worked. Words refused to form. Like a heavyweight boxer sucker-punched me, I actually doubled over.

"Goddamn it, *Jen!*" Jeff whirled around to face his sister. He never let go of my hand, but his voice was far off now.

My ears were ringing, the top of my head screaming from the ring blow. That's what we used to call it, anyway. Jim wore a ginormous Native American silver ring with a beautiful bright turquoise jewel in the center. I always found it so ironic that he hated the people but adorned himself in their jewelry. He'd turn his hand palm facing up and strike you hard on the top of your head with that ring. I swear to this day, I still have a knot on top of my head from his repeated assaults. The blow was strong enough to bring my four-year-old body to my knees. I'd forgotten to close the chicken coop the night before after feeding time, and now at 6:00 a.m. all the chickens were scattered around the farm. Such an indiscretion was not tolerated, and I should've known the blow was coming. On my knees, the gravel cutting into my bare skin, I apologized repeatedly hoping an early offense would diffuse his anger. I was wrong.

Jeff was facing me now, his mouth was moving, but I didn't hear his words.

"*You're dirty! You're ugly!*" come Michelle's words.

The feeling returned to my legs and I bolted back to the safety of Jen's bathroom. With the door locked, I sat on the edge of her tub. I heard Jeff on the other side of the door, pleading for me to come out. My face was burning hot, and the top of my head was throbbing. Was that possible? Can you conjure up an old physical wound from a new emotional wound?

The questions barrel down at me like a runaway freight train. Why would she say that? How is one word so crippling? Is that how she's felt all along? How many times had she asked him that question in the eight months we've been dating? Does his mom or grandmother feel the same way? Despite all the hugs and family dinners we've shared, do they call me a nigger when I'm not around? How many times had Jeff heard his family say racist shit? What had his response been?

I, of all people, knew that you can be in a room and folks feel totally comfortable slinging racist slurs like patties on the grill. She had moved from Lake Havasu to Phoenix, but Jen was raised in that close-minded town. If there was barely any diversity now, Lake Havasu had to have been stark white when she was growing up. Clarity begins to dawn; Jen is a racist. I'm dating a man, and thinking about a future together, who has racist family members.

Jeff apologized the entire three-hour drive home. I cared so deeply for him and I knew all he wanted was for me to be happy and he'd do everything he could to protect me. We survived that incident. I chose to forgive the situation and attempted to move on. The final blow to our relationship, for me anyway, happened on a different weekend trip. This time it was Flagstaff, Arizona. It's a medium size town in northern Arizona. Beautiful, mountainous, and also not known for its diversity. What is it with this state? We were meeting my parents for one of my mom's infamous weekend craft shows. Craft shows were like a religion to my mom. They were highly revered and above reproach. Creativity ran deep in the veins of the Panno women. From knitting delicate baby blankets to sewing giant embroidered wall hangings, those women created as a second language, adorning all of our houses with their artwork.

My mom and my sister had such a fractured and often estranged relationship, that when my dad wasn't being coerced into tagging along, it was me who was volunteered as her artisan show plus one. Did I mention that I cannot create to save my soul? Maybe my particular DNA cocktail wasn't creatively conducive. Either way, craft shows never excited me. I agreed to this one only after Jeff wisely convinced me. He said it was a perfect opportunity to play tourists in Flagstaff, a town I'd yet to visit.

The show was set up in a park venue. A beautiful crisp fall day, the trees were in their glory displaying the full autumn palette. The artist's tables sat end to end weaving throughout the park, a veritable wedding aisle. By 10:00 a.m., the eager shoppers were in full swing, visiting each table, perusing the endless array of one-of-a-kind wares, pottery, paintings, and exquisite jewelry.

Per my mom's instructions, we were to divide and conquer. She was in the hunt for a particular co-creator that she'd heard was a vendor there, and that we, the non-artistically gifted, would slow her down. The resignation on my dad's face when she pulled his arm to join her, was priceless. So, Jeff and I were on our own.

It wasn't until the third time it happened that I started to pay attention. Slowly walking hand and hand through the crowds, I couldn't help but notice when I'd look up from a vendor's table, I'd catch someone staring. At first, I thought I imagined it. I honestly didn't grow up being admired. My mother never learned how to do my hair, so I didn't have bad hair days, I had bad hair years.

Growing up, I always assumed I was ugly. No magazines or commercials ever celebrated my hair or features. I wasn't used to anyone paying attention to me. It was disconcerting to have people stare at me. Then I realized they weren't only looking at me, they were gawking at both Jeff *and* me. First at me, then at him, then back at me. As if they were trying to piece a puzzle together.

Jeff looked up and followed my gaze to one unhappy looking man standing next to what I'm assuming was his wife. She was feverishly picking through a display of turquoise necklaces. The man locked eyes with me and gave a disapproving smirk. I watched him shake his head.

"That's disgusting," he tsked as he motioned with his forehead toward Jeff and my clasped fingers.

Simultaneously, Jeff and I glanced down toward our hands. In his defense, maybe Jeff was as confused as I was. Maybe he thought the man was referring to something gross on the ground. But whatever went through his mind was irrelevant to me, because he dropped my hand. Left it there, dangling alone. Abandoned. To face this bigoted man's judgment of our relationship.

I walked away. I was done.
I couldn't do it anymore.

"I don't want to fight this fight!" I called out at the heavens, loud enough for people to hear, but to no one in particular.

If and when I decide to get married, it will be to a Black man and we will raise Black children and live in Black neighborhoods and the children will attend Black schools. I may not be able to end racism or bigotry or change history, but I will at least fight the battle with someone who understands my anguish.

CHAPTER 16

My life seemed to turn on its head during my weekend jaunts. Technically, this time it was a Monday night, but you get the idea. Over the upcoming 1992 holiday break, my cousin Tina and I planned to spend our New Year's Eve together.

As far as grandkids go, Michelle, my sister, is the oldest. Then there are four of us cousin girls. First is Kimberly, born February 7 to my mom's oldest younger sister, Sharon. Two weeks later, Tina is born February 21 to my mom's oldest younger brother, Frank. A year later, in April, I am born. Finally, Leah pulls up the rear as Kimberly's younger sister on September 23. There are a dozen more younger grandkids but the four of us girls grew up thick as thieves. The close proximity in age meant we were discovering life and unlocking its mysteries simultaneously. We learned how to put on makeup together, cuss together, like boys together, and inhale cigarette smoke (without dying) together. We looked out for each other. We all assumed the term kissing cousins was named for us. As we've gotten older, Tina and I have become the closest. She is one of the dearest people to me and I love her immensely. She is sweet and kind and generous, which is why what happened was so painful.

I met Michele in remedial math class at Mohave Community college and we became instant friends as we struggled to get through what was supposed to be the "easy" math class. She was sweet and loud and possessed an endless amount of energy. Tina and I decided to invite Michele to come to California and go out with us on New Year's Eve. Michele loved to dance too and would complete the trio perfectly. We'd stay at Tina's parents' house and on New Year's Eve, hit up the hot local dance spots. After hours of shopping for the perfect dresses, we reconvened in Tina's bathroom and spent only the kind of hours girls can, getting ready. Two hours of makeup and twelve outfit changes later, we were ready for the big night.

Tina and Michele were both fourteen months my senior, and even though I was only twenty, I had a fake ID granting me access into all the bars. Technically, it wasn't fake, it just wasn't accurate. See, what had happened was... I loved to dance and during the time I was living in Havasu, I was lonely. When you're under twenty-one, there's very little to do in a small town. I missed dancing so much. My mom's best friend's daughters had temporarily moved to Havasu as well. The girls were two years older than me and could get into the one bar in town that had a dance floor and a weekend DJ. The music was great and I longed to go and dance with the girls. For months my mom had watched me mope around the house on weekend nights alone while the Murray girls went out. I think the guilt of moving us to Havasu was still on her heart. That guilt softened her heart to play an accomplice in my scheme.

It was 1990, the tiny town's Department of Motor Vehicles' office was run by an elderly couple who argued more than they worked. Their documentation system was antiquated. They still hand-wrote most of the forms, leaving a dusty IBM model computer abandoned on a corner desk. I never could figure out how that office uploaded to the state's system. This also worked to my game plan's advantage.

On a Monday morning, I walked into the DMV, with my mom no less, and presented my older sister's birth certificate as my own to obtain a license. Apparently, we had interrupted that morning's argument. I was glad for the distraction. I was nervous and certain everyone could hear my heart pounding. The wife informed me there was to be a written portion and driving portion of the exam. While the husband graded my written test, my mom kept peppering him with questions about his upcoming fishing trip. He was so excited to brag about what he was destined to catch, that he never had a free minute to question why me, a supposed twenty-seven-year-old, had never once applied for a license before. I played right along though, feigning exaggerated fishing intrigue whenever there was a pause in his story. In less than thirty minutes, that elderly couple helped me secure a driver's license without a second glance. A benefit to that small town I shall never forget.

As you hold this book in your hands, somewhere in the annals of Lake Havasu City's database, there is a driver's license with a picture of a brown-eyed and very brown-skinned (it was summertime, and I was super dark)

Michelle Panno, a normally super fair-skinned blonde with blue eyes. Don't judge. We all have a past.

The agreement was simple; my mom would help me secure an ID as long as I didn't drink when I went out. It was a perfect arrangement because truly all I wanted was to dance. Besides, I'd done enough drinking in high school that my liver was on strike.

Armed with my fake ID and dressed to the nines, the three of us hit the road in pursuit of the hottest guys and best New Year's Eve party. The night didn't go as planned though. We made it to one spot that was a complete dud, the music was whack and the small crowd wasn't much better. Making matters worse, not one hot guy was to be found. After only forty-five minutes, we retreated back to Tina's Camaro. We'd been driving for over an hour and all of us were frustrated. This is a pre-cellphone, pre-Google, and pre-Yelp era. There was no quick check on social to see where the hot spot was that night. We had envisioned a jamming club scene, music so loud you could feel the bass reverberating in your hips, partying, hours of dancing, and some hot guys' tongues down our throats. We'd talked about it for weeks now. But none of that was happening.

It was nearing midnight and our nerves were getting short. We had yet to find a spot. I was riding shotgun and suddenly we drove by a spot that looked perfect. There was a line out the door, the music was jamming so loud we could hear it inside the car. Even the people in line were having their own private party, dancing with each other, laughing, and carrying on. They looked like they were having a blast and I wanted some of that.

"There! That's the perfect spot! Let's go there. Our search is over ladies!" I yelled out over the club's music.

"*No!* That's where all the niggers go!" Tina shoots back as she drives past the club.

Stunned, I stammer but can't make my mouth form words. It feels like something has pierced the inside of my heart. My mind does that spinning thing again and the world goes into slow motion. Her words are so unexpected: like a betrayal.

The bile in my stomach rises into my throat and the bitterness finds its way into my mouth. She knows the truth. I told her what my mom had revealed. She had been the one person I trusted. Tina doesn't share my Black DNA, she doesn't know my struggle, but she has always been a true friend, always the steady in my corner, sympathizing when I cried over my mom's betrayal. But now her words seem foreign. As if someone else, some enemy, had hurled them at me. Like a sniper's bullet you never see coming.

Reeling, I was looking for solid ground to land on. Wasn't she the one who was so hurt when her father refused to let her go on a date with a boy she really liked because he was Black? Her father said,

"No daughter of mine will ever date a nigger."

Finally, acidly I said, "You know that's what I am, right?"

The car went silent.

Did I notice everyone in line was Black before I suggested we stop? Is that what enticed me? I cannot say for sure. I'm always the *only* one in any party we ever go to. I have always been the *only* one in my family. I'm the *only* one who always has to make the adjustment, the concession. Did I subconsciously think that for once, the scales would be flipped? That this one time I'd be the one in the majority? With people I feel at home with. I stared out my window and slowly the line of would-be patrons moving to the music's rhythms, passed out of my sight.

We stayed silent. Never giving voice to the pain or what I assumed was my cousin's shame. Did her outburst surprise even her? Was she consciously aware of her own bigotry? We were of the same family, but we were not the same. Tina kept her eyes focused on the road ahead and I stared but did not see out my window. For her part, Michele occupied the backseat awkwardness that's bred from desperately trying to avoid other people's family drama. We chose instead to let the radio cover up our deadened words.

We did end up finding another club, a white club, that night. Just before the clock struck the bewitching midnight hour, we wedged ourselves onto an obscenely packed dance floor, melding our bodies to the beating rhythms. Then we yelled out the countdown alongside the nameless crowd.

I'd spent a lifetime keeping inside feelings inside. This night was no different. On the outside, my lips smiled. I used my voice to yell "Happy New Year" to perfect strangers. Inside, secretly my heart reinforced protective walls insulating me from future thoughtless and cruel verbal attacks. I reminded myself that sometimes wolves are dressed in sheep's clothing.

CHAPTER 17

I don't know how to be two people. I don't know how to meld two opposing world views, two identities that are contrary to each other by nature. Black versus white. The oppressed versus the oppressor. They are diametrically opposite, yet they both live within me. I am new to the idea of blackness as an identity. Sometimes, I don't know how to ride this invisible line.

I didn't grow up Black, so I miss the inside jokes, the "you had to be there" references. What they mean is you had to be Black to understand. And yet, I can no longer be white. The world does not view the twenty-year-old adult me as white or as some version of passing for white. I am definitely "other" to them. My unruly dark curly hair is just the first clue. My hips and booty won't lie, and they won't pass.

My super power is I am oppositional by nature. I defy rules. My contradictory personality gives me my edge. Tenacity runs through my veins. It was either that or wilt under the first assault dished out seventeen years ago from my sister. Everything since has thickened my outer layer, the bullying, the "where's your mommy?"

from strangers while I'm standing right next to her in the neighborhood park.

That tenacity came in handy when I figured out that there would be no welcome wagon from Black students for me. I don't know what I expected when I arrived on USC's campus but whatever it was, it definitely wasn't ambiguity. People believe the opposite of love is hate. That's wrong, it's ambivalence. It's the "you don't even register on my attention radar" disposition that dejected me. If I'm being honest, I hoped that I'd finally been seen and accepted. I was eager for a warm welcome into a community. Like "You're one of us. Welcome to our tribe." Maybe that's why I clung to the idea of joining a Black sorority. I just wanted a community of Black women who would embrace me. How was I to know that colorism would cast its ugly shadow on me, claiming my dreams as yet another victim.

The Black student population at USC was less than 4 percent, and yet it didn't feel like that to me because I had surrounded myself with Black student life. I became a member of the Black Student Association (BSA). I attended all the Black Student Union meetings. I almost exclusively hung out with other Black students and attended every Black event. When Angela Davis, Maya Angelou, Cornel West, or Nikki Giovanni came to speak, I sat in the front and center row.

I consumed Black culture and the problems that plague Black students as if they were my major. Yet even in this small community, I was still an outsider. Campus life was a microcosm of the larger world. The Black male students were happy to see another brown girl on campus, albeit a very light-skinned brown girl. This created a rift between me and other darker skinned girls that I did not see coming. You have to remember that I didn't have the background that breeds understanding. I naively believed all Black women, young and old alike, wanted to be my friend and that just wasn't the case. The hard lesson I'd yet to learn was the serious emotional and psychological battle of prejudices among Black people.

Prejudices based on skin tone, with a marked preference for lighter-skinned people, is another casualty of colonialism. In this country, colorism is the toxic aftermath of chattel slavery. Decades post-slavery, when everyone was theoretically free and a citizen regardless of race, discrimination raged on against individuals with dark skin. The one-drop rule meant that white people could maintain social and economic control. It also meant that the closer you were to white the more you perceived yourself successful or at least there were more opportunities to become successful.

"If you is white, You be alright,
If you is brown, stick around,
But if you Black then get back"

Like many other nursery rhymes and childhood stories, we are conditioned by what gets repeated most. Colorism is not just an American phenomenon either; skin bleaching cream tragically is a highly sought after product in many African countries. Throughout the world, self-mutilation to achieve a whiter appearance is prevalent. Self-loathing based on repeated stereotypes and the accepted standard of beauty is real. What I also didn't know at the time was that the girls who were hating on me, most likely were battling their own self-hatred, passed down for generations.

By the end of my sophomore year, I had completed three semesters and had enjoyed being involved with campus life. Then the president's seat in the Black Student Union became vacant. I wanted the position. I believed I could do a great job in the role. I loved the idea of bringing about more positive change for Black students. I was inspired to serve, and I was tired of living invisible. Simultaneously, I was terrified by the idea of campaigning and opening myself up to the criticism.

"Who she think she is?"

"She ain't Black, not really."

They think I didn't hear them, but I did. Three young ladies from the sorority I did not end up pledging gathered at the end of the conference table we had all just adjourned from. They're not the only ones. They all think I didn't see the eye rolls when I spoke up. They think I didn't notice when they grabbed their boyfriend's hand when I walked into a room or passed them on the yard (that's what the Black students call the part of campus where they congregate) as if I'm some type of Jezebel who came to steal their man.

The BSA meeting topic had been about whether the organization should sponsor Chris Rock returning to the campus for another show. I'd seen his show my first semester and I thought it was garbage. I liked him as a comedian, but his off-color jokes that night were disgusting and weren't funny. Yeah, I said it. He was terrible. I don't hold a leadership role, so I don't get a vote, but I did voice my concerns when the president opened up the floor for comments. I was in favor of funding an upcoming summer literacy program for the local elementary school instead. It had not been a popular position.

I knew those girls weren't the only non-fans of mine, which felt hurtful. Hadn't I marched with all the other Black students when it was exposed that the university admissions weren't giving equal treatment to Black applicants? Hadn't I protested for better housing? Wasn't it me who stood with them and advocated for more inclusionary policies? What else did I have to do to be accepted? It isn't as if I get to go back to being white. No one is checking for me in that camp anymore. Here I am again. Still not good enough.

This is all I can be, Goddamnit!

Other than Nikki, I hadn't made close female friends. I had many associates but not true female friends. An interesting trend was emerging, however. The majority of my closer friendships were male. No one would've ever accused me of being a sports fan, but four of my closest friends played football and basketball, respectively, for the university. I couldn't talk shop, but we studied together, acted silly together, and laughed a lot. There was just an ease and no weirdness with my male friends and certainly never any of the competitiveness I'd felt from my own gender.

Yet, four friends do not win a presidency seat. I vacillated for two excruciating weeks, surrendering sleep for long nights of tossing and turning. The thought of campaigning felt like laying down and exposing my underbelly to a pack of wolves.

In the end, after a pep talk from Nikki, who now was in pursuit of her own career since graduating, I decided to take the leap and run for the seat. Nikki, as my "campaign advisor," helped me from afar to secure the resources I would need to make what seemed like hundreds of posters, banners, and flyers. Literally over one weekend, we plastered the campus with "VOTE FOR BARB" signage. You couldn't travel fifty feet in any direction on that campus without being assaulted by my election crusade.

"Go as big as you can!" was Nikki's advice. "Don't give 'em any reason not to know your name."

Meanwhile, I kept my Black university life secret from my family. My family had no idea of the life I was leading just sixty-five miles west from them. I had grown up feeling invisible and now I was struggling to live out loud. Mostly, I didn't know how to meld the two worlds, the two identities in my mind. It all felt so complicated. My response: I told no one. No one at USC knew my family was white and I kept my white family in the dark about becoming super Black.

CHAPTER 18

I won! Shortly after winning the BSU presidency, summer break had arrived. I was staying on campus for the summer. No identity resolution or metamorphosis had befallen me yet, so instead of spending the hottest months of the year in hell, or Lake Havasu (whichever you prefer to call it), I decided to remain in Los Angeles. Besides, I figured I was giving everyone in my family a break from my blackness. I know my mom specifically was having the hardest time with my identity shift. I am certain she never imagined, or maybe she never allowed herself to imagine, that one day she would have to tell me who my real biological father was, and I would respond with a full emergence into Black culture. That one day, she would no longer be able to relate to me, her own daughter she had once shared her body with. Me, who seemed foreign to her now. Me, who she used to share daily phone calls with but now our calls were getting farther apart. Me, who she knew she *never* could prepare to be a Black woman in America.

My summer plan was simple, I would work and use the break to plan BSU's calendar for the upcoming academic year. Campus life was pretty quiet during the summer and I knew I could get a lot accomplished. I had speakers to schedule, personal assistants to coordinate with, meeting agendas to write out. We would be collaborating with a local youth group to sponsor a New York City art museum trip and there was an endless list of to-dos for it. The other BSU cabinet members had all left for the summer, so I was on my own. Periodic phones calls served as our check-ins.

I was also relieved at the break from girl drama. If I'm honest, I wanted to prove the naysayers wrong. That they had judged me wrong, that I *was* capable. That I *was* Black enough. My mom may have robbed me of knowing my true identity growing up; I may have lived a lie, but the truth was out, and I was here now. I was fully embracing being Black and stepping up into a leadership role. Something inside kept beckoning me forward, kept demanding that I not live small. I was scared but doing it anyway. It would be a long time from that moment before I stopped being afraid. The blessing about being young is that you don't know what you don't know.

I had hoped in this new role, Black students would see me, truly see me. Instead, I was still being held on the outside, even if only slightly this time. Yes, they accepted me as a Black student, but almost like I was on a trial basis, a legit ninety-day probation type of shit. I was frustrated by it, but I refused to let anyone see that. It helped that Secret deodorant had been running a commercial that cautioned women to *"Never let 'em see you sweat."* I embodied that slogan. It helped that I had an ace named Nikki in my pocket. She gave me great counsel, having done the exact same job two years earlier. Her guidance that summer inspired me to create an incredible lineup of upcoming events. Despite the questionable support from the other students, that summer I proved I was worthy of the position.

I read recently about a biracial woman who went searching for her birth parents and found out she was an African princess; she was literally *royalty!* Not the "I come from kings and queens, my brother." She was actually born to a Sierra Leone tribal king! My truth was very different, I never met my biological father. Never had one Black family member embrace me. I had to navigate these unchartered waters solely on my own, blindfolded.

I can only speculate, as my mother never confessed her truth to me. Maybe she felt shame that she'd committed adultery with a married man who already had children. Maybe it was a fear of losing me. Whatever her burdens were, even after she revealed her lie, she did everything she could to thwart me from finding him. This man who had contributed half of my DNA; this man who changed her entire life.

Steeling myself, "What was his last name, Mom?" I asked one arbitrary day when I was nineteen.

I had been working up my nerve for months to ask. After that fateful day my senior year, not one word had been spoken about my biological father. As if her only responsibility was to tell me he was Black. I had been blessed, we had all been blessed, the minute Art Navarro came into our lives. Prior to him, my mother's picker had been off, always choosing the defective guy. Art, my true Dad, was everything a man, a father, a human should be. He had been doing the job so he earned the title. I was grateful for him and the life he helped my mom create for us. I never wanted it to appear that I wasn't grateful for him. But my love and gratitude for Art did not quench my longing to fit in somewhere.

Silence.

"Where was he from?"

Silence.

When it was clear I wasn't going to accept her silence she said, "Oh honey, it was 1970. All the entertainers were changing their names. His last name probably wasn't even real," came the only response I ever received. And that, ladies and gentlemen, was a wrap. The subject was closed.

———

I was about to enter my junior year. I had accomplished many things I had set out to do, getting accepted and beginning school at USC, getting active within the Black student organizations and now, landing a leadership role. Yet, I was still searching. Like an itch you simply cannot reach, no matter how hard you try, your arm is just not long enough. I had the feeling that I was missing some aspect of myself. I had heard so often that college students go through a phase of trying to find themselves and maybe this was it for me, yet somehow, I doubted that.

"When the student is ready the teacher will appear."

I'm pretty sure Buddha wrote this quote for me; it is my fundamental and universal truth. Teachers are the facilitators of change, and over my life, they have always shown up at the exact crucial moments I needed them most.

As a student organization leader, you work closely with the Office of Student Affairs. The director of Student Affairs at USC was Dr. Lonnie Anderson, an incredibly kind, supportive badass with enough street smarts to teach his own master class. As a Black man, he believed it was his responsibility to uplift and support Black students on campus. Representing only 4 percent of the student body, he made it his mission to advocate for our organizations. That summer was no exception. Planning BSU's calendar required a lot of coordination with his office. To this day, I don't know if it was really true that he had hours of free time or he simply frustrated his secretary to no end when he would sit with me for large chunks of his workday. It seemed no matter when I showed up, he'd clear a path for me.

Dr. Anderson was patient as I navigated this newly acquired role of governance. He gave me insight and guidance. He would use humor to take the edge off his advice. Sometimes, he had to full stop put the brakes on my overly ambitious attempts to lead. He'd remind me that a good leader is a good follower first and listens more than she speaks. After weeks and weeks of spending so many hours together, a trust was built. I confided in him about my family being white and about recently "becoming Black." A year into our friendship, I even confided about the molestation and cried for nearly an entire afternoon, sitting at his little round table in his office as he patiently doled out his sympathy.

"Oh honey, that is awful," and "I am beyond sorry you had to endure that nightmare."

Outside of Nikki, who had been off campus for six months, Dr. Anderson was my biggest supporter and became a true friend. I will forever be in his debt for showing up as the perfect teacher for me in the perfect moment.

During my time spent at USC, I didn't observe a specific faith. Although I had been raised Catholic, that transitioned into "loosely" Catholic by middle school when my parents were going through their own religious internal struggle. We would attend mass on all the big holidays and pray over our dinners, but for the remainder of the year, we were pretty much heathens. Ultimately, after I graduated from USC, they converted to Protestant Methodist and became bible-quoting, door-knocking, zealots in pursuit of winning over souls. I was spiritually committed to God; I simply could not sign onto the dogma of any one organized religion. Religion was another topic my family and I debated for hours but simply could not find common ground.

Three years had passed since first reading X's autobiography. Three years of learning the truth of the transatlantic slave trade, chattel slavery, and Jim Crow laws. Three years of fury so ferocious it was blinding. Three years of scorn toward white America. A bitterness and revulsion for the criminal justice system that criminalized blackness. Then the fury began to fade to anger. Yet, there was still something missing. Something else had to exist besides even anger. I was still searching. My personality is that of a doer; I needed to do something. Randomly, one Saturday morning, I decided a church service was the answer. I may not have known what was missing in my heart, but I believed God did.

The following morning, in the bedroom of my apartment I shared with another USC student, I stood at the ironing board pressing a dress for the service. The radio had been on as background noise until I heard the words,

"Have you ever believed there was something beyond your anger?" My ears caught those words as if the morning show DJ had just tapped my on my shoulder with a *"Pssst."*

I paused, breath held and my hand mid-iron stroke. I stood still so long awaiting the radio announcer's next words that I nearly scorched my dress.

"Black people! Do you want to empower yourself, lift your community up and learn the true power of where we come from?"

I was mesmerized. I hadn't realized that I was holding my breath until he said,

"Then you need to attend the Awake Lecture Series!"

"What is that? And *yes*, I do!" I answered the radio voice back.

"Our culture has been stolen. We did not come from slaves. We are descendants of the first people. We created the arts and sciences. We have been *miseducated* to see our individual and collective reality through the prism of white supremacy."

Her voice was melodic, measured, and insistent. Her passion seized my heart, and I knew, in that instant, I would do whatever it took to be at that lecture series. Her name was Eraka Rouzorondu, she was an Afrocentric Black revolutionist and the creator of the program she was describing.

The beauty of preparing yourself, being open, willing, and available is that your efforts are rewarded, and the teacher will appear. For nearly two years, I hadn't been to a church service, I had never been an early morning riser, ever and listening to the radio wasn't really my thing. Yet, that morning God had answered my silent prayer, the one I hadn't even realized I was praying for. I was up, I was headed to church and listening to the radio. All so I could receive my blessing. As soon as the show ended, I called Nikki and informed her, not asked, that we, she and I, would be at the Unity bookstore that Tuesday night for the Awake Lecture Series overview.

On Tuesday night, Nikki and I learned that the advertised course was thirty-eight hours long. It would take place over the course of the following week and would be held at the bookstore we were sitting in. The cost was $238, and I had *no* idea how I would pay for it. It was the beginning of the summer and I hadn't secured a summer job yet. Also, since it was summer, the dorms were closed, which meant I had to move off campus and pay rent. Somehow, none of that worried me. Certain a way would be made, Nikki and I pinky promised that we would be there beginning next Monday, no matter what.

Over the course of that next week, I'm not even sure how to describe that transformative evolution that unfolded within me. My soul was stirred in a way that I would never be the same. In a way that a butterfly will never again be a caterpillar, I was never going to be the version of Barbara who was absently listening to the radio on Sunday morning.

The lecture series was not an easy one. There were volumes of material covered and a never-ending reading list. During class time, you just had to buckle up; Eraka spoke fast to cover the massive amounts of content. Emotionally, it was also difficult. The students came to lean on one another as we banded together as the lies were revealed. I sobbed during the class on the transatlantic slave trade, gasping for air during the slide show depicting the belly of the slave ships carrying humans as cargo chained to one another shackled with barely enough air to breathe; stacked on one another so inhumanely that it was nearly impossible for my mind to accept that such an atrocity could have been committed by other humans and for *four hundred years!*

By the third day of class, the slide projector was protesting. It made this loud clicking sound each time the slide advanced. The class chronicled the actual beginnings of architecture. My mouth literally fell open in awe at the magnitude of the structures we had historically built. I watched overwhelmed with pride as images of the Great Pyramids flashed on the large screen. Astounded, I learned that in nearly five thousand years, no amount of advanced technology had ever been able to replicate the structural precision of the engineering.

CLICK

The image of The Mali empire so rich through trade that by the fourteenth century it was the source of nearly half of the world's gold exported from West Africa. (Lynch, 1978)

CLICK

The Kingdom of Kush, home of the Kushite capital of Meroe and home to ruins of over two hundred pyramids. (Bennet, 2021)

CLICK

Eighth century Carthage, the North African commercial hub with a massive economy based on textile, gold, and silver trading. Carthage was a seafaring empire, with a half million residents with docking bays for over two hundred ships that rivaled ancient Rome in the Punic Wars. Hundreds of years before the lies that Christopher Columbus was the first to sail the seas, when the Europeans still believed the world was flat, Carthagians were sailing to South America and Asia on *two hundred ships!* (Ashante, 1983)

CLICK

The Songhai Empire, a fifteenth century West African empire, where King Askia Muhammad established hundreds of Islamic schools in Timbuktu and held open court to scholars and poets throughout the Muslim world. (White, MacDonald, Grierson, 2021)

There were countless dynasties of ruling kingdoms throughout the entire continent of Africa that I never knew existed. (Adams, 1983) Dynasties that created and supported global trades and economies. Universities were erected that taught advanced sciences, mathematics, and written languages when Europeans were still cave dwelling in the dark ages. (Bennett, 2021)

Anger, as familiar to me as the wrinkles on my hands, hardened in my throat. It felt like I swallowed a bite of food whole. No history books, no world cultures classes, no news stories *ever* taught me or anyone else about the magnificence of Africans.

"They stole our history!" was my seething outburst in class.

Nadra, a fellow student, laid her hand on mine to steady my trembling.

"I know, honey, I know." Tears were streaming down her cheeks. I listened to the sniffles around the room. Watched the others comfort one another, trying desperately to share the burden of the pain.

It was as if I was outside of my body. Anger. Resentment. Fury. Lies! My mind is whirling. Calculating the years of lies, the years of deceit. All my life, hell, all of our lives, we've been lied to. Africa was the beginning of civilization! Not the country of uncivilized subhumans. Not where 3/5 of a man originated from! Africa was the birthplace of all knowledge, where the Universities of Enlightenment taught Hippocrates and Socrates, where religions were conceived, not the other way around. White folks in this country had been burning the descendants of kings and queens alive in their demonic lynchings!

Then, out of nowhere, I began to laugh, not a giggle but a full-bellied, hearty, nearly hysterical laugh. I knew I looked like a crazy person. Like someone on the brink of losing her mind and maybe I was.

"They stole our history," I said again, choosing my inside voice over my previous shriek.

Nadra pressed her lips to my hand she held clasped in hers. I believe the mother in her was trying to shield me from the pain.

The origins of science and mathematics are credited to the Greeks, Romans, or other European whites. Those are *lies!* For hundreds of years, Europeans have stolen, then systematically erased, Africans as the original people by culturally appropriating their wisdom, education, and advancements as their own. Furthering the insanity, Europeans, the original students, then made all attempts to destroy their master's empires. They tried to erase the evidence of ethnicity, the noses and the hair on all the statues were destroyed.

Clarity for me began to soothe the anger. Yes, invading a land vastly rich in all resources (minerals, metals, and humans) and slowly bleeding it to death; then brainwashing its inhabitants to believe they are less than human, is a travesty beyond imagination. And strangely, there was beauty in now fully understanding from whom I hail.

They were not slaves, they were not 3/5 of men, they were the original people. I, then, AM a descendant of royalty.

Lulling the anger into pride, I am beginning to find my way on a much-needed journey to peace.

CHAPTER 19

The Awake Lecture Series impacted me in such an unforeseen way. What I had expected was to be moved, but not in a way that I was unable to continue in the same life direction. I entered USC ambitiously pursuing a declared Political Science major. Pre-Awake Lecture Series, I was driven and laser focused on my meticulously designed plan: graduate USC, apply and be accepted into NYU Law School, then move to New York and complete the journey to becoming a high-powered attorney with a prestigious law firm. Post-Awake Lecture Series: Not. One. Single Part. of that plan would I ever pursue.

I was so sickened by the five-hundred-year reign of terror against people of color. The indisputable truth: propaganda and racist policies created the trillion-dollar prison industrial complex and mass incarcerations imprisoned 1/3 of all Black men, rendering intact Black families extinct. There was no peace here for me. No alternate universe where I could avoid the madness. I refused to be complicit. The turning point happened when I learned about the history of the police. It was my monopoly moment. You know, that moment when you cannot pass go, you cannot collect your $200 and you definitely cannot keep playing.

The advent of policing and their purpose was never to protect and serve neighborhoods, keeping them safe from potential criminals. The advent of policing was called Slave Patrols, created in the late 1600s and employed in 1704. They were groups of armed white men, first used in the Province of Carolina (later becoming North and South Carolina). Their only job was to prevent slave rebellions, especially on the plantations where resistance was the greatest. The patrols were tasked with serving land and plantation owners and politicians by capturing, torturing, and returning (if they survived) the enslaved Africans. (Hassett-Walker, 2021)

Policing the movements of enslaved Africans, the patrols sadistically enacted barbaric public whippings and lynchings for even the slightest indiscretions so as to never allow their prey to gather and plot escapes. Policing the movements of Black people, slave patrols were explicit in their design to empower the white population. Slave codes and other punitive legislation were enacted to control and restrict all movement. They grew in popularity and spread throughout the thirteen colonies.

The invention of the cotton gin increased the greed and a demand to enslave more Africans. As day follows night, so rose the fear of rebellions. When you enslave human beings, keep them against their will, you must always, by default, live in fear that one day they will revolt. I agonized over the question, is this at the heart of why white America, hundreds of years later, cannot allow a truly free and just society for all to exist? Is it the constant fear of retribution? Is that the source of the proverbial boot on Black America's throat? Or is it something far more sinister?

From its inception, law enforcement has created laws and policies to legalize and legitimatize hunting and murdering Black people. How could I be complicit in this system? If I ignored history, I would betray all of whom had lost their lives at the hands of white tyranny. I was twenty-one, grew up in the suburbs of white America, and even I knew young Black men were rotting away in prison for crimes their white counterparts had been slapped on the wrist with probation for.

For every "War on…" Black people suffer. War on poverty, war on drugs, war on crime.

The federal government funnels tens of millions of dollars of federal aid and paramilitary equipment to state and local law enforcement agencies willing to wage the wars. The Reagan administration revised the Edward Byrne Memorial State and Local Law Enforcement Assistance program to legally offer massive bribes to states to amass an inmate population for profit. Tripling budgets can be a very convincing motivator for politicians. Essentially, it pays to play. Cumulatively, almost inconceivable sums of tax dollars are reallotted to building the largest prison industrial complex on the planet. Mass media images are created and marketed that perpetuate stereotypes of people of color and poor people as criminal, delinquent, and deviant. Those domestic wars serve up longer, harsher sentences on nonviolent Black and brown people, imprisoning one out of every six (currently, one out of five) Black men. This destroys Black families, reinforces ghettos, and defunds public school systems, amputating possibilities, perpetuating gang warfare, and paralyzing

Black economies. This country has been engaging in a war on Black people since 1492. (Alexander, 2020)

Slavery is alive and well today, it's just been redesigned.
I simply could no longer participate.

This new revelation uprooted me, ungrounded all of my plans. My decided path torn from me like the thousands of families torn apart on the auction blocks of the antebellum south. *What in the hell was I going to do now?* I was attending a primarily white academic institution that had no investment in uplifting people of color. There were no fields of study offered by USC to aid me on my quest to become a change agent, no African American studies major, no Pan African studies, and no ethnic studies of any kind. *No nothing.*

The veil of the greatest country in the world inexorably exposed, I stood naked. Vulnerable. Implacable yet clueless as to what to do next. Looking back now with a life of learned wisdom, I could've chosen to pursue civil rights law. It honestly never occurred to me that I could still become an attorney to advocate and defend against the injustices committed daily against people of color. Instead, at that time, for my own sanity, I needed to put an entire universe between the law and me. I contemplated quitting school altogether. When I considered my journey to get here, I ultimately dismissed the idea.

Seemingly out of nowhere, an idea began to coalesce in my mind. If I had to stay at this institution and seek a degree so I could empower my people and the university didn't have what I wanted, I would simply create my own. I would petition the University board of directors, imploring them that I wanted my own major.

My confused academic counselor responded with,

"Why on Earth would you want to do that? You are less than eighteen months from graduating."

Then, when he couldn't dissuade me, he simply said it wasn't possible. It only takes meeting me once to know that if you tell me I cannot do something, please know that is *exactly* what the hell I'm about to do. It took a dozen nos and more "why do you want to do thats?" than I can recall, but in the end I prevailed. I was given permission to create an "Ethnic Studies" major. Essentially, because there was no precedent for it, there was little oversight and nearly no advisement. So, I simply found all the Black professors on campus and enrolled in their classes.

I spent so much time in the film school taking classes that it was assumed I was a film student. I was not. Dr. Todd Boyd, a.k.a. "Notorious PhD," was the most dynamic, controversial, conscious Black professor on that campus and I couldn't get enough of his classes. At only twenty-nine years old himself, he was a rising star at USC's film school. He taught the Introduction to Film courses, but my view of film was forever changed in his Black Film course. Dr. Boyd never shied away from a difficult conversation. It is probably more accurate to say he instigated them. He challenged his students to think beyond the political rhetoric. He purposely colored outside the lines and demanded his students meet him beyond the borders, beyond their comfort zones. We'd watch films like *The Spook Who Sat by the Door, Superfly, Dolemite, Shaft,* and *What's Love Got to Do With It.* The class would be all fired up from the blatant stereotypes and discrimination and Dr. Boyd would pour lighter fluid on the fury and fan the flames. Some of the best conversations I had on that campus came from those classes.

Armed with my new major, my new direction, and my new plan, the downward spiral halted and I felt freer than I had in recent memory. Free to pursue a new dream. I didn't have it all figured out, far from it. What I did have was my integrity back. I no longer felt like an imposter, rather 1993's version of Kathleen Cleaver of the Black Panther Party or political activist turned Marxist, Angela Davis.

CHAPTER 20

You are no longer capable of holding the same worldview after attending the Awake Lecture Series. It destabilizes you, thirty-eight hours of dislodging your hold on your former beliefs, an undeniable Neo's red pill, blue pill Matrix moment.

The things that once meant so much to me, paled in comparison to my newly held beliefs, and as such, I no longer was enthralled with the men I was dating. I had dated a few students during my first semesters but ultimately wasn't impressed. Then I dated a few of my professors (don't judge, I appreciated the wisdom of older men), and while I could learn a lot from them, what appealed to me right then was a shared experience of becoming conscious. I wanted to go on dates and talk about reparations, our government's conspiracy to silence any Black resistance, why the status quo must be destroyed, and why it's even necessary to call them Black Revolutionaries.

Eraka was hosting a new class, Conscious Dating: An Afrocentric Approach to Male Female Relationships. Once again, I dragged Nikki there, hoping Eraka would reveal some secret to finding the perfect guy. Nikki, walking by my side as we entered, was still fussing at me. She'd been mad since we got in the car. We were late, per my usual. For her part, Nikki didn't know how to function unless she was fifteen minutes early for everything. Her training came from her stepfather, a retired military vet, who would leave you if you weren't in the car fifteen minutes early. Then there was me. The most foreign thing to me is punctuality.

I had no idea that a man already seated in the audience had looked up as I walked in and told his best friend sitting next to him that I would be his wife one day.

That man, seven years my senior, was Jerry Cartwright. A handsome, twenty-nine-year-old former music student turned academic advisor for The International School of Music in Hollywood, California. He was the son of Victoria Cartwright, a woman who I would come to love and revere, and Jerald Cartwright who had passed years earlier. Jerry was the fourth of six children, and he was close with all of them. He grew up in Topeka, Kansas and had the slightest hint of a lisp when he spoke.

He was kind and gentle and could speak about the theoretical and practical application of music with such a severe passion you couldn't help but be swept away on its current. We didn't actually meet for another two months. Eraka was hosting a Friends of Ascension Productions meet and greet. All of the alumni of the multiple lecture series she had taught were invited to gather, break bread, and share ideas on how we could continue the work she was doing. At that event, we formed committees and committed to raising funds enabling Eraka, a DC resident, to continue traveling to LA. Our goal was to empower as many Black Angelinos as possible by awakening them from their slumber.

Jerry, who had attended the lecture series a couple weeks after me, was assigned to the marketing committee along with me. Less than a week later, I was dropping off flyers for him to duplicate at his job. He was very proud of the school he worked at and gave me an extended tour. A quick drop-off turned into over an hour visit. That coming Friday, the school was hosting a live concert of some hot new band. Jerry invited me to come and that began a six-month friendship. We spent hours talking on the phone about the work we were doing, my new major, his music, and how to solve institutionalized racism.

In early January 1994, I was at his job again, this time picking up some needed documents for our group. As we were walking down the hall, we were talking about the group's upcoming potluck dinner and, without warning, Jerry took my hand into his. My heart skipped a beat then fluttered rapidly for over a minute. I was nervous and felt sure he could hear the roaring thudding in my chest. My cheeks started tingling, and when I reached up with my free hand, they felt warm. I wanted to seem calm, cool, and mature. I mean he was seven years older than me, but on the inside, my stomach was doing summersaults. I looked up at him, and when he smiled, I relaxed my hand in his. When we reached the end of the hallway, he asked me out on a date.

It was a small Italian family restaurant not far from his house in San Fernando Valley. The intimacy of the tiny, candlelit, cloth-lined tables and Claudio Baglioni serenading us through the speakers felt like the most romantic night I'd ever had. We talked and ate and talked some more. The waitress, encouraged by our appetites, kept up a steady pace of small plates of rigatoni, pesto alla genovese, lasagna, and spaghetti. We talked almost nonstop, barely taking time to chew. I'm certain the food was delicious, but honestly, I couldn't swear to it. Instead, I remember feeling that my heart had found its place. I think we were the last to leave the cozy little cafe.

Standing in his driveway at the end of the night, we were holding hands and gazing up at the stars. I remember it was so quiet, only the chorus of crickets disturbed the silence. Then quietly Jerry said,

"I'd like for you to be my wife."

I giggled, assuming he was joking. I mean, it was a lovely dinner, but it was our *first* date. However, when I turned to face him, there was no humor to be found. He shared what he had told Soleh (his best friend) the night he first saw me. He told me he had been looking for a woman just like me. He knew about my family. We had talked about them months ago. I had shared then that I was still distancing myself from them and trying to figure out who I was independent of them. Hell, I was trying to lay my own foundation. For my part, at twenty-two, marriage wasn't on my mind.

He was undaunted and simply said "In time, you'll see."

Little did I know, we'd be married by March.

CHAPTER 21

Over the next two months, Jerry and I were inseparable during our free time. We spent a lot of time sneaking in phone calls while he was at work and he patiently listened to me as I shared my challenges with my family. My frustrations with my mom not understanding me. My hurt and betrayal at all of them. He was supportive and not overly opinionated, and only gave advice when I asked for his input.

He, along with Nikki, wanted me to confront my family. I was living this whole separate life from them. I was operating in the world as a Black woman, as a whole Black woman. Not half of a Black woman. I was not living as a biracial woman, whatever that even means.

And therein lies my problem.

I do not know how to be half of anything.

I am ambitious. I have grown into a driven goal-oriented person. I don't know how to half-pursue something. Give me a cause and I'm all about it. Ten toes in, I go hard in the paint. Both Jerry and Nikki kept reassuring me that it was time to sit my family down.

I dreaded this. I avoided this idea like the plague. I could only think that it's *me* who's the giant elephant in the middle of the room. Me, that my family and I had been tiptoeing around for twenty-two years. We don't touch it, we don't name it, we don't acknowledge it. A fucking thirteen-thousand-pound African elephant had been in the middle of the goddamn room for twenty-two years and *not once had we named it*! It had pressed us against the walls, prevented us from seeing one another across the room. It had given us the false illusion that it would go away but it hasn't. In fact, the elephant is expanding. It is taking up more oxygen, threatening to rob us all of needed breathing air because I wasn't going to stop being me.

Finally, the tension became too much. My avoidance was no longer serving me. I hadn't told my family I took the Awake Lecture series nor about my inner struggle and ultimately changing my major. If I continue on my own path of denial, I am no different than my family. The elephant was stealing my oxygen now.

My cousin Tina got married a few months back and I was her matron of honor. For the occasion, I had my hair braided into a beautiful crown, its regal elegance atop my head made me feel like an African queen. I showed up the night before to the rehearsal dinner ring in nose, hair coiffed with a whole Black attitude. My family was struggling, I saw it in them, I felt it. They don't know what to say to me. I was also becoming aware that this "thing" is for me to resolve. I cannot depend on them to fix this. This was my lesson, maybe it always has been. Maybe the Universe was always waiting for me to get to this moment to find this place in my heart, my place in the world. No one else can walk my lessons for me. I see that now.

I picked up the phone to call my mom, then paused. The receiver actually felt heavy in my hand. It's almost like the phone was forewarning me. I dialed the first three numbers by memory. I paused again for so long the busy signal began chirping loudly at me. I hung up the phone. I paused again. This was so much harder than I hoped it would be. Confronting the past, naming it, naming me, and who I was in the world today.

Almost like a surprise, I hear myself out loud begin to say the things I needed to hear in that moment:

"This is necessary. You can no longer wait for something to change. You are strong. Your family loves you. They will keep loving you even if you tell them out loud how you feel."

I took a deep breath and began dialing each number slowly, feeling the hard plastic of each button under my fingertip. I heard the ringing begin and instantly I wanted to hang the receiver up.

This must happen, I thought. *You can do this.*

Her voice on the other end sounded surprised. My calls had become less and less frequent and we just talked a week ago. Our conversation had been brief then; she had asked how my political science classes were going, I couldn't bear the conversation about my major change months ago, so I said nothing. Another illusion that must be unveiled. Tonight, I kept it light and said: "I'd love for us all to have a big family dinner."

Other than holidays, those dinners had become less frequent. Maybe because we kids were getting older, scheduling had just made it hard. Either way, now I was calling one. My mom agreed. I think I heard some trepidation in her voice. Does she suspect I had news? Does she know change was coming, that it was inevitable? Was her mom intuition alarm ringing? I could practically see her incessantly wringing out her hands as if she's holding that water-soaked rag again.

If any of those were true, she offered no confirmation, no resistance other than the nervous tension I detected. It's settled, next Friday at Olive Garden. Of course, it's Olive Garden, we're Italian after all, *"when you're here, you're family."*

I asked Jerry to come with me; it will be the first time he would meet my family. If he was nervous about it, he didn't let on. I think he knew this night was already a lot for me and he wouldn't burden me with his own emotions. He wouldn't give those to me to carry as well.

My family lived a little over an hour away. The drive felt more like five. There was a clock on my car dashboard; I'm certain it was broken or maybe time had just stopped. Instead, I began to count the exits, until even those fail to mark time accurately. As if time had somehow tricked us all, or maybe it's just me. Has it always been me? Have I always experienced time this way, or was it only in moments of emotional turmoil?

Of course not, you're being ridiculous! I hear the voice in my head clearly. She sounds judgmental.

"I don't know what is happening," I responded.

"We're going to meet your family," Jerry said patiently. He thinks I was talking to him. I did not correct him.

Every exit passed adds to the countdown.

You're dirty! You're ugly!

Another exit. My anxiety was mounting.

Your name is not Grace!

My chest tightened and my breath caught in my throat.

Another exit.

Oh sweetie, you can't play Cinderella, she doesn't look like...

Another exit.

Jerry put a reassuring hand on my thigh. Could he see I was struggling? Could he hear the voices? They seemed so loud.

Three niggers walk into a bar...

Another exit.

Where's your real mommy?

My eyes burn and I feel the tears sting as they trickle down my cheeks, slowly then without ceasing.

Another exit.

You know you want this. You know you like when I touch...

Jerry's voice was faint, as if it was far away, like the distance between the two front seats are miles apart. I think he's reminding me that this was the right thing to do.

Another exit.

We're gonna show you what we do to nigger girls.

Another exit.

She's not really Black.

The voice in my head grew louder. She's nearly screaming now, a veritable shriek.

We are so close now, only five exits away. The pain in my chest won't relent. I've spent my whole life believing a lie. First, it was believing my sister's venom, then believing I was unlovable, then that I was unworthy, that Jesse's violation tainted me, then that I'd never be enough.

"Enough! It's fucking enough!" I shrieked back at the voice.

Jerry is startled. He doesn't really ever curse, and I've never heard him yell. But he hadn't heard the taunting voice sabotaging my peace. I have had enough, I am sick and tired of everyone else defining me, limiting me, condemning me.

Four exits away.

I get to choose how I want to live. Who I want to be. I get to define myself for myself.

Kujichagulia.

The word drifts into my thoughts like a light summer breeze. Then it nestles into my heart, and I feel the resonance of truth. Kujichagulia is the second day of Kwanzaa. Kwanzaa is a week-long celebration honoring African heritage in African American culture. Kujichagulia means self-determination. To define ourselves, to name ourselves, to create for ourselves, and to speak for ourselves. The seven principles of Kwanzaa were in response to the 1965 Watts Riots and the civil unrest leading up to the riots. Black people needed to reclaim their ancestral pride and celebrate their culture and history. Befitting, as it feels as if I have endured my own riot and this dinner, this reclamation of my own identity, was my response.

We are exiting now, only a couple more minutes. I am ready now.

As if the restaurant knew my revelation needed its privacy, they sat our dinner party in a large private room. Dinner was nice. The food was delicious and comforting in the way that only Italian carbs can offer. It's so good to see my whole family. We laughed and joked and told family stories. Jerry was a big hit. I'm not sure what I expected, but my family was welcoming. A few members were not in attendance. Neither my sister nor my brother were there. I am okay with that though. Independently, they both have spent the past two years wreaking all manner of havoc on their lives. Drinking, drugging, and running from their problems. I wish so badly that both of them would make different choices, but I'm learning that I have zero control over that. I see their absence was taking a toll on my mom though; I could feel her sadness.

As the dishes are cleared away and the servers exit the room, I took one last deep breath. For the past ten minutes I have been counting down each place setting being removed. I knew it was time.

You could just not do this. I hear my thoughts and for the briefest of moments I fantasize about excusing myself to the bathroom and setting off the fire alarm. In high school, I had the same fantasy during every final exam that I hadn't prepared for. Just me?

This time I ignore the thought. This is my time and I am doing this.

I stand. My stomach is doing flips, but my knees are strong, unwaveringly supporting me. I feel strong. Everyone looks up at me, expectantly, and I smile.

"I love each and every one of you," I begin, taking the time to travel the table's circumference to look each of them in the eyes.

"I have always loved you. I have always accepted you for who you are." I continue, my stomach relaxing as each word passes my lips.

"I have seen each of you for who you are, and not asked you to be different. Not asked you to be other than what you have claimed for yourself."

I take a deep breath. All eyes are on me. There isn't a sound to be heard outside my voice, even the younger cousins are listening raptly. I had thought of almost nothing except this night for weeks and yet it occurs to me that I have not prepared one word of my "speech," so I don't know everything that I am going to say. This is so typical of me that I nearly roll my eyes at myself. They do not know what is coming, of that I am certain.

I tell myself that I need to say the next thing. That it must come from me. That this is my truth. That they must hear me say it.

"The world sees me as a Black woman..." another slow deep breath... "because I am a Black woman."

Did I find it odd that no one appears confused? Not even the little cousins? Questions flash in my mind.

How many conversations have been had about you that you never knew about? How many times has your family had secret conferences about you? Was it after strange looks from the doctor's appointments my Aunt Barb used to take me to? Or when the Olan Mills photographer assumed I belonged to the other family that had come to the studio because they were Black? Or when my Uncle Paul had to come pick me up from school when I was sick and the teacher didn't believe he was my uncle?

No one is surprised. I continued before I lost my nerve. They have known all along. Of course they have. All the family portraits with the one chocolate spot. All the summers when I would tan three shades darker, no sunscreen ever needed. While all my cousins suffered from awful sunburns. All the tangled hair combing that my cousins' brushes would never work on. When in middle school, after our whole lives of sharing everything, I couldn't squeeze my hips into their jeans anymore. Of course they all knew.

"I need for you all to continue to be there for me. To accept me. But for who I am. Not what you want me to be. I am a Black woman. Yes, I am also Italian, but I cannot be a white woman. The world does not see me that way. They see me as a Black woman, and I am good with that. This is my truth now. I can only be what I am and live my truth."

Finally, I need to make this last request. To create this bridge for myself. One last deep inhale.

"I need for you all to love me as me and not want me to be anything other than me. To love all of me exactly as I am and for whom I am today."

Then there's this collective sigh. It's audible. I hear it. Were they always waiting for me to speak this truth? My eyes well up in tears, not the sad ones though, not the pained ones, not the "why can't you just see me" tears.

The tears of relief, the tears of finally. Finally, settling into my own skin. Finally, not needing to apologize for my hair, my skin, my thicker lips, for my hips that refuse to be white. Finally, to be enough.

Afterward, there are hugs from everyone. Affirmations of love. Reassurance. Then I exhaled. *Twenty-two years of tension escapes with my breath. Joy is what is left. I am good with that.*

CHAPTER 22

Ironically, not long after that dinner, I started feeling very ill. For weeks, my exhaustion level had inexplicably risen to an all-time high. Yes, I was taking a full class load and was active on campus and working and participating in Friends of Ascension, but this was different. I had no idea this level of tiredness was possible. Consumed with fatigue, I could barely drag my body out of bed each morning. Then I fought to stay awake all day long. Collapsing back into bed at night was such a huge relief, it felt euphoric. I swear that feeling was better than an orgasm.

Finally, one lazy Saturday afternoon when I still couldn't force my body into action, Jerry nudged me and kissed the top of my head. We'd moved from my bed to the couch and I had been laying quietly in his arms for a while. Jerry looked down at me and asked, "Could you be pregnant?"

Several times over the past two weeks, he had suggested I go to the campus health center for a checkup. I knew he was concerned, and his worry was endearing to me. I, however, am the hardhead my mother always said I was and believed I could just tough it out. It was probably some passing virus that just needed more time. I'd be fine.

So, when I heard him say these words, my world spun. I lifted my head off his chest with my response.

"Absolutely not!" I said, louder than I had intended and with much more conviction than I actually possessed.

"Think about it, baby. It would all make sense."

"*No*! It does not! I'm fine!" Now I know I'm lying, but to whom? Me? Him? I do not know. What I do know is that I do not want to be having this conversation.

"Listen," he began super gently as if he's speaking to a caged lion. "Let's just get a test and rule it out." His voice is soft and measured like he's trying to coax someone down off of a ledge.

Maybe I am on a ledge. Because what he's saying can't be true. I haven't planned for this; translation, I am not controlling this. I have learned that hard-headedness is code for control freak. Having only had to witness my mother as the matriarch in my family, synchronizing her five siblings, her parents, her husband, and her children's lives. Expertly navigating the pitfalls like an award-winning orchestra conductor, my mother kept a tight control on everything she could in her life. I observed this, I respected this and I embraced the idea that happiness came from controlling all aspects of one's life.

So much of my life growing up was not under my jurisdiction. I wanted, nay, I needed, to control my adult experiences.

This was a definite sharp turn in my path I had not seen coming and couldn't figure out how to control. Jerry's calming encouragement is what got me off the couch, into the car to go purchase a home pregnancy test and back home peeing on a stick. The test instructions read: wait five minutes for accurate results. Laying back on the couch, my exhaustion reclaimed my energy. When the timer went off, Jerry looked at me and I nodded. He knew it had to be him who went and looked. It had to be him who led.

Walking back into the living room carrying the test applicator, he was genuinely smiling. A joy I hadn't seen on his face before. I knew the answer. I knew he had always wanted to be a father. Always wanted a family. He knew on our first date, or maybe it was when he first saw me, that it was me he wanted as his life partner. If he was scared, he never showed it. He only walked over to me, put his arms around me and kissed me.

"What am I gonna do with a baby?" I whispered, scared.

"Love it." Was all he said, utterly convinced that life was truly that simple.

I, on the other hand, was terrified. Thinking about my own childhood and the fact that my mom had had three kids and I was the only one who turned out. The odds were simply not in my favor. Hell, I was still trying to figure myself out, how could I be a good mom? I was extremely self-centered. My life and all my decisions only had to consider me. I was in my senior year. A baby meant a radical shift in my life plan, albeit if I'm honest, that plan was in flux these days.

The truth was, I questioned my own ability to keep a child, my child, safe from the world's pain. Back and forth I argued with myself, playing both sides and feeling battered and bruised at the end of each match. In the end, the one truth I did know, the one thing I could not argue with was that I loved Jerry deeply. I knew in my soul he would be a phenomenal father and partner for life. I knew he would keep his family safe no matter what the cost was for him. I trusted that when I didn't know the answer, he would.

It helped that Tina and her husband were also expecting their first child. Although Tina and I were living totally different lives, I cherished our relationship and somehow her going first gave me courage.

Because the Universe is kind, the blessings began pouring in. I had made a friend, who lived in a neighboring community, during the lecture series nearly a year prior. Jentz created the most elaborate and beautiful personalized natal Astrology charts for clients. One night on a break from class, Jentz had shared one of her drawings. Intrigued by having my own astronomical snapshot of the stars based on the exact time of my birth, I booked an appointment with her.

I remember her porch had been on the top level of her three-story home. My back to the front door, I admired the neighborhood down below with its giant green oak trees and perfectly manicured lawns. It was late afternoon and the kids were outside playing, their laughter floating up to where I stood. While I waited for Jentz to answer my knock, I had absently thought what a wonderful street to raise a family on.

A year later, I wanted to share my incredible chart-reading experience with Jerry. Standing at his side on Jentz's porch, Jerry and I marveled at the view. The sun was setting and the LA breeze had chilled the spring day down considerably. He put his arm around me to ward against the coolness.

"This seems like a wonderful family neighborhood," Jerry observed.

Seated together inside her beautifully decorated living room, we admired the traditional African art and paintings covering the walls. The three of us spent hours that night visiting one subject after the next. Not only had Jentz completed Jerry's chart, but she also created an overlay of both of our charts together and told us of the great adventures we would have together. We shared a knowing smile, a secret smile. It was so new that we had agreed to not share the pregnancy news yet.

Toward the end of our visit, Jentz shared that her mother, Lola, known to everyone as Mama Lola, was currently in Ghana building a house and would return home later that year. Jentz had said her mother, the community midwife, had recently retired and her office studio downstairs was vacant. Mama Lola had used it for over thirty years caring for pregnant moms. My ears perked up. Jentz saw my interest and asked if we'd like to see the studio. Once downstairs, she unlocked the door, then excused herself saying she was needed upstairs, winked at me as if she'd been in on the secret the whole time, then turned and walked back up to her floor.

Perplexed, I walked inside, Jerry following me. It was a small one bedroom, one bathroom studio with hard wood floors throughout. There were giant windows everywhere that gave it the perfect warm and welcoming feel. Moonlight gleamed in through the front picture window creating dancing shadows of the leaves on the opposite wall. It was a perfect little place, nestled on the first floor surrounded by beautiful ivy and shaded and protected by a ginormous oak tree.

We had finished touring the small place, looking through glass kitchen cabinets and admiring the tiniest pink bathroom I'd ever seen. It was adorable and perfect. Standing outside again, we admired a perfect moon. Right there, on that little step- up porch hand in hand, Jerry got down on one knee and once again asked me to be his wife.

We no longer believed in European-based traditions, and we rebuked church weddings. Thanks to the education of the Awake Lecture Series, Jerry and I had condemnation for all Judeo-Christian holidays. The early American Christian church was proslavery. It sponsored slave ships, perpetrated and prolonged the human slave trade by using the bible to justify the horrors of beatings, rapes, family separations, and lynchings. They claimed enslaved Africans were descendants of Ham and thereby their subjection was fitting. Illegalizing literacy for those chained and bonded kept them ignorant and unable to properly refute the lies.

A church wedding was out. Hell, I felt so rebellious those days that I wanted no part of what I was calling a slave master's society. Instead, we created our own spiritually-based commitment ceremony. We chose a full moon and in the backyard of the house Jerry shared with his roommates, all alone, we made promises to God, the ancestors, and to each other.

A month later, we both moved out of our roommate situations into Jentz's studio. Each day, the pregnant fatigue was slowly improving, and my impending graduation was giving me tremendous joy. It was a spring graduation, but because I had changed my major, I would have another semester of classes. I chose to walk early, in the spring, then get a full-time job and finish my final coursework directly with my supervising professor. It was all planned perfectly; the baby would come just after finals. I'd be ready. Except life is rarely ever perfect.

My wholistic, granola side really developed during my pregnancy. I wanted to expose myself and my unborn baby to the healthiest things. In part, this was due to Eraka's last class in the lecture series. It was all about creating the best health. You can't be woke and sick at the same time. A conscious sick revolutionary does no good for the cause. The day she taught that class was the day I became a vegetarian. Almost a year to the date of my one-year anniversary of her class, Jerry and I asked her to be the baby's Godmother. She graciously accepted and vowed to always provide spiritual guidance to our baby his whole life long.

We took raw cooking classes, visited the farmer's market every Sunday for the freshest vegetables and drank blue-green algae. After work, we walked the streets of our perfect little neighborhood and practiced prenatal yoga poses together in front of the beautiful picture window. Honestly, we were a bit disgusting with all the pregnant joyful happiness, but we didn't care.

We attended a birthing class with a certified prenatal instructor and after learning of her background and experience, we were impressed. But it was her African- centered approach to birth that sealed it for us. We hired her to be our midwife. Her name was Ma'at, she was newly pregnant with her fourth baby and had three beautiful little chocolate drops already of her own. I loved her immediately. Her husband, Tehuti, and she hosted the weekly classes in their home and I grew to love their entire family. She eventually became my best friend and inspired my career choice to pursue midwifery.

Jerry and I planned to have our baby at home with Ma'at. We prepared for six months, explored all of our options. We studied everything we could get our hands on. We purchased all manner of birth things including a full home birth kit stocked with all the medical supplies needed. I ate extremely healthy and took excellent care of myself. I went to all my prenatal appointments with my doctor, concluding at the end of each appointment that the baby and I were strong and healthy. We had an emergency backup hospital. We were birth-ready.

CHAPTER 23

The thought of becoming an actual mother was daunting to me. I had the theoretical knowledge about mothering, but no idea how to successfully mother. How does one go about winning the gold medal for motherhood? I'd been babysitting since I was in third grade. I knew my way around infants, and not the easy kind of babies either. I could cloth-diaper a screaming, fussy, feverish baby in record time, safety pins and all. I could soothe an over-tired, colicky, teething baby back into a slumber without breaking a sweat. It wasn't the task of keeping a baby alive that I feared. It was raising a healthy human with all my own shortcomings that terrified me.

This is what brought me back to my mother. This woman who had the equivalent of a PhD in sociology life experience. She had practically raised her younger siblings and went on to have four kids of her own beginning at the age of sixteen. While she had her own frailty and imperfections, I had no doubt that my mother loved us deeply. I may not have agreed with all of her choices, but I believed my mother had done the best she could with what she had, even when the outcome was bad.

Somehow experiencing a life developing and growing within me, sharing my body, hearing its rhythmic heartbeat over the Doppler fetal scope, and feeling the kicks and movements of this tiny human, I met my mother. I could see her now. Not with judgmental eyes, but with compassion. Not with pain, but with empathy. Not with accusations, but with grace. The closer my impending birth loomed, the more I grew. I finally saw my mother for the flawed but loving spirit she had always been. She hadn't changed, I had.

We became close again, my mother and I, bonding over my burgeoning belly. I called her every day. I had a jillion questions about my changing body, what to expect with birth, how to heal naturally, and why I couldn't maintain my own emotions to save my soul. She answered each of my calls no matter the time of day and even at night when I couldn't sleep. She was patient with me, she calmed my anxieties and reminded me that I didn't need to know everything about raising a teenager just yet. That all I had to do right now was bring life into the world and love this little precious one. One day at a time, she kept reminding me.

When Jerry and I made the decision to have our baby at home, I was nervous to tell her. I assumed she would try to talk me out of it. Claim some "safer at the place where dying, diseased people went to be treated" reasoning. Instead, I was floored when she said, "I had both you and your brother in the car on the way to the hospital with Jim driving and no help at all. I'm certain I would've been happier at home." Shocked and relieved that she was so supportive, I was invigorated.

The day I went into labor was such a surprise. We weren't expecting baby for another two weeks. Clearly this baby was not taking its punctual cues from me. It was November 29. We were expecting a mid-December baby. I had been feeling Braxton Hicks (pre-labor contractions) for a week now. Racing to complete my finals with a contracting uterus while trying to keep a baby inside my body, who is incidentally tap dancing on my bladder, was not fun, people!

My mother, who lived ninety minutes away, had hosted a baby shower a week prior and all the gifted baby clothes were at her house to be washed. She and my dad would bring everything to us on the upcoming weekend. Which is to say, there was not one piece of baby paraphernalia in our home the day my contractions started.

I worked on the fourth floor of a Beverly Hills office building. When the pains in my abdomen got to the point that I could no longer ignore them, I took the elevator down to the first floor and walked a bit hoping they would go away (I think I had read that somewhere). I wasn't ready. I kept reasoning that I could make them go away. No surprise there. They didn't.

My boss brought me home claiming I'd be a hazard on the road. I went directly to bed, midwife's orders. At 12:22 a.m., a contraction jolted me out of bed like a butcher knife to my abdomen. I tried walking the short distance to the front room where Jerry was strumming a beautiful melody on his guitar. I hadn't even crossed the bedroom threshold when another contraction hit and dropped me to my knees. Jerry rushed to me and knew to call the midwife. He never left my side again. For two hours he breathed with me, supported me, soothed me with cool damp lavender cloths (Twenty-six years later, it's still my favorite scent.).

Ma'at showed up at 1:45 a.m., albeit a bit battle worn from another birth that night, and seven months pregnant herself. I remember apologizing saying,

"I'm sorry to disturb you. This is probably just a false alarm."

The contractions were less than two minutes apart. Ma'at gave me that "oh honey, you have no idea, do you?" look. I was delirious, but I didn't actually think it was labor. I mean, how would I know; I'd never done it before. I was sweating profusely. There was this internal raging inferno that was burning my body up from the inside. I had disrobed entirely and was on my knees desperately holding onto the only thing I believed would support my very pregnant body. It was the tiny little sink counter in the tiny little pink bathroom. Ma'at begged for me to come out. Jerry begged for me to come out.

I refused.

"The bedroom is all set up for you in here." They pleaded in unison.

I refused.

I couldn't leave my beloved counter. I wouldn't abandon the only thing that understood my pain. I was irrational and didn't give a *damn*. Then the most explosive menstrual-like cramp I had ever experienced, consumed my entire body. My vision went completely tunnel, all sound disappeared, and the breath left my body. Molten lava fire ignited in my vagina. The labia inferno felt like a violent grand finale at a Fourth of July fireworks show. I surrendered. Released any illusions of control I had over my body and I bellowed out the loudest guttural animalistic moan from the deepest region of my soul.

Later Ma'at would tell me she had instructed Jerry to step over me and stand inside our bathtub. She then had him squat down and with his arms, grab under my armpits and pull me into a squat. The moment I was in the squat, a viselike urge devoured my entire being and the only possible response was to use inhuman strength to bear down. With gymnast-like agility, Ma'at wedged her own squatting, seven-month pregnant body in the fourteen-inch space between the toilet and the wall, to catch the emerging baby. The baby came out in a gush with one huge push. He came so fast, I was so low, she couldn't guide his head out slowly to prevent the tearing flesh.

Somewhere very far off, I hear Ma'at saying: "Barbara, you did it! It's a *boy*!"

But my arms instantly were too heavy to lift. The adrenalin from my superhuman feat waned, replaced by extreme weakness that enveloped my body.

Then when I didn't respond, "Take your baby, you did it. Take your son!"

Maybe it was Jerry who put the baby in my arms.

But there was the blood...

It was a fourth-degree tear. Ma'at couldn't assess to verify if the laceration had ruptured through to my rectum. The tiny pink tiles were disappearing under the hemorrhaged blood. I was losing so much blood. Too much.

My vision went tunnel again and I watched her mouth move but I couldn't understand the words she was saying. I couldn't make my mouth work to tell her as much.

Darkness.

How long did I hold the baby for? A brief moment? Longer? Maybe, it was longer.

Darkness.

Everything moved like molasses on a cold winter day. I couldn't focus. My eyes disobeyed my command to stay open. Ma'at was yelling now. I'm not sure what she was saying though. Jerry's face got very close to mine. He was asking me something. No, telling me something, but I was so tired.

Darkness.

I just wanted to rest. My head was too heavy. I tried closing my eyes again. He was shaking me now. Hard.

Why won't they let me rest?

The ambulance sirens were loud.

Its only 2:45 in the morning, I remember thinking. *The sirens will wake all of our neighbors.*

Loud sounds accosted my ears. I was laying on a hospital gurney. More yelling. Only this time, it was a nurse pleading for Jerry to give her the baby, saying she needs to run tests on him. But the baby was perfect. What tests? He hadn't cried once. He was calm, peaceful, and alert. Ma'at had thoroughly examined him after he was born. An eight-pound healthy baby boy with no issues. He passed all the newborn screening assessments with flying colors. Our home had been very peaceful and welcoming. He was never in any distress.

My head was throbbing. I closed my eyes again.

The staff was in an uproar. The harsh fluorescent lights glared down at me when I reopened my eyes. The clamoring of a dozen mechanical machines bounced off hard surfaces and echoed throughout what appeared to be a wide hallway.

Why are we in a hallway?

Jerry was standing about a half dozen feet from where I was laying. He was holding the baby who was swathed in...

Is that our bath towel?

The beeping of a nearby patient's heart monitor machine was almost like white noise. Suddenly, the sounds of urgent shrilling bells two doors down called out.

"He's coding!" someone yelled.

Sounds of rubber-soled shoes scurrying past us in the direction of the alarms. Who's ever in charge was calling out dire orders. I looked back to see Jerry shaking his head violently as someone approached him with their hands outstretched.

The lower half of my body was cold. No, it was numb. My head throbbed, but the loss of feeling in my legs scared me so I lifted my head slightly. My legs were exposed. I was wearing Jerry's black Miles Davis T-shirt, the one with the bleach stain at the bottom that I've begged him to throw away. Ma'at must've helped me into it before we left. I have no idea how she managed with her round belly, but I was also wearing underwear. They were saturated in blood now though and the white covered gurney I'm lying on had slowly turned a dull red under me.

The unknown patient's code emergency averted, and the hum of the ventilator machines came back into range. The week prior, I had read that anywhere from 90 percent to 99 percent of alarms that go off on inpatient units are false alarms. The staff become alarm fatigued and dulled to their impact. Yet for patients and their families, those false alarms cause stress and launch them into fight-or-flight responses. We all know that stress is bad for our health. Reason number 623 that we had wanted a home birth.

The two nurses standing nearest to Jerry insisted on admitting our perfectly peaceful and healthy baby boy. They claimed we were neglectful parents. For thousands and thousands of years, women birthed in their homes with trained midwives. Technology and intervention do not equate to healthier outcomes. Birth trauma for babies and mothers are real, morbidity rates for postpartum women of color in this country are staggeringly high. This was unacceptable to Jerry and I. We had made a well thought out, well researched, and educated decision. Our choice was anything but neglectful.

I watched the theatrics around me unfold like a melodramatic *Telanovela* episode. Only everything was still in slow motion. Or maybe my mind was working so slowly. I knew something was very wrong, yet I couldn't make my mouth ask for help. The exhaustion was overwhelming. The effort was too great; I could not move a muscle in my body. My head had lulled off to its side. Again, I glanced down the gurney. This time I watched the blood, my blood, drip onto the stark white tile floor.

The security guard was now trying to pry the baby out of Jerry's hand. Ma'at is yelling.

Drip. Drip. Drip.

Fatigue gripped me. I closed my eyes. Not even during the first trimester was I this tired and weak. I just wanted to surrender to the sleep that was beckoning, to let go.

Drip. Drip. Drip.

"Barbara! Stay with me! Stay here! Your baby needs you!" Ma'at was yelling at me now.

When I didn't respond, she turned to the nurses standing by watching Jerry yell at the guard who was now trying to pry our baby out of his arms.

"For God's sake! Will someone *please help her!*"

Drip. Drip. Drip.

The pool of my blood on the floor was spreading. I closed my eyes again. I was so tired. I just wanted to drift off.

Child Protective Services had been called and a social worker was standing near my gurney, trying to avoid getting the blood on her shoes.

"Ma'am, did you plan on having your baby at home?"

I know my answer was supposed to be no. California does not support home births. I was supposed to say no. I couldn't think clearly. Everything was fuzzy. I couldn't keep my eyes open any longer. I surrendered and felt like I was floating away.

"*Help her now!*" Ma'at exploded, and this time someone listened.

I was wheeled off. Two interns finally cleaned me up and repaired the torn flesh so the bleeding would stop.

Hours later, with my newborn son nestled next to me in an actual hospital bed, in an actual room, we waited. Jerry had to take the social worker to our home so she could verify for her file that we, in fact, had prepared to have a baby. That we had the essentials to take care of said baby. She also needed to speak with my mother to verify this information. I was a twenty-three-year-old married woman, and my mommy had to validate my readiness to be a mother. The irony wasn't lost on me.

In the end, my son gained his name from the whole ordeal. Never, not one time, in the over eight hours that we spent in that hospital, through the commotion, yelling, the grab attempts, alarm bells, and not eating for hours did he ever cry. He was awake the entire time. He was observant, steadfast, calm, certain, and had purpose.

They whispered to him,
You cannot withstand the storm,
He whispered back,
I am the storm.

CHAPTER 24

Words have energy.

Names have energy.

The names we give our children will be repeated countless times throughout their lifetime and that energy is bestowed upon them each time their name is spoken. Knowing this, Jerry and I believed a child's name should be chosen for its meaning. That meaning should come from observing the child.

Who is he? How does he behave? How did he show up in the world? What do we wish for him?

We celebrated on the seventh day after my son's birth with a traditional African-naming ceremony. It is taught that those seven days are sacred. It is a time for bonding, a time for learning, a time of gratitude for the blessing bestowed upon the new life.

Naming a child is a sacred rite of passage. The traditions of a naming ceremony are to announce the birth of a newborn and to introduce the child to his extended family and greater community. Ceremoniously conferring the name upon the child, the elder in the village traditionally conducts the event. There are meaningful rituals that everyone in attendance participates in, and of course, afterward we break bread with one another. *As African*

Americans who cannot trace (or at least not in the 1990s—think pre-Ancestory.com) *our heritage to a specific village or tribe, we must embrace an entire continent.* In doing so, Jerry and I included several elements representing many African countries in the ceremony.

Like most parents, we spent months thinking about baby names. We wanted to choose a name that would bestow the best of this little one's potential. Giving him roots and wings and inspiration to fulfill his purpose here. True to our nature, Jerry and I researched book after book on African names and their meanings, so when the time was here, we'd be prepared. We took the entire seven days to choose the baby's name and, observing tradition, we never spoke the names out loud. It is custom to infuse the name with blessings on the day of the ceremony, as a reveal of sorts. Dressed in beautiful African garb, the three of us drove to Ma'at and Tehuti's home, where Tehuti would be the master of ceremonies. All of our friends would be in attendance.

Neither of our families would be, however.

Jerry's family all still lived in Kansas and the distance was too great to travel on such short notice. As for mine, they were not invited. I know how this sounds. Let me explain. In my heart, I loved them all dearly and yet I still had not found the place where my two worlds could coalesce. I lived an African-centered life in Los Angeles, donned in African clothing, hair braided, wearing my baby on my back swathed in African material, surrounded by a beautiful group of like-minded Black families. To my family's credit, since the dinner, when I would visit, I felt their easing into my blackness. They were all doing their best to be accepting of me. Even still, in my heart the worlds were distinctly foreign to one another. *So, for the time being, I made peace that the two worlds would remain apart.* A veritable separate but equal.

Opening the ceremony, it is traditional to call on the ancestors, to pray for their guidance for the newest member of our community. Tehuti asked for permission from the elders in the room to speak, mindful to always acknowledge their wisdom and offer them our respect. It was a beautiful ceremony full of symbolic elements to bless the baby. We spoke of our experience bringing this little life earth-side. Then, the moment everyone had waited for arrives. The eldest man in our village was a Nigerian man; he stood to confer the name of the baby, speak of the meanings of the name and introduce the baby to his new extended family.

Instead of concluding the ceremony, however, he said he felt called to bestow a family name upon us.

"I am inspired by your pursuit of your ancestral culture, your commitment to raise your family with their heritage and giving your children a foundation of knowing where they come from."

"Olatunji of the Yoruba tribe, means honor reawakened. I believe you have become reawakened and with honor."

Only then did he hold our son up and call out his full name:

"Kamau Agyei Bakari Olatunji."

Quiet warrior. Messenger of God. Of noble promise. Honor reawakened.

———

I sat at the kitchen table. The kitchen is the heart of the house for Italian families. No matter if it is the smallest or most cramped, no matter if that the living room has all the comfy furniture. The kitchen is the place where we commune. Food is nurturing. It feeds the soul and my family will feed you, no matter what the occasion is.

That particular afternoon's visit to my Uncle Frank's home, I was sitting alone at the table. Sitting solo is a rarity; there's always a cousin or two milling about. My Aunt Barb was standing at the counter preparing dinner. My back was to her, her rhythmic movements of dicing random vegetables stopped. She walked over to me and took a seat next to mine.

"I came across something that I believe should be yours." Her words felt ominous.

I was unsure how to respond.

Hesitantly, I said, "Okay."

She headed up the stairs to her bedroom and when she returned, she was carrying a picture. I couldn't see it yet; the picture was pressed to her stomach. When she sat back down next to me, I felt the weight of her emotions.

"I think it's time for you to see your father."

I let the newspaper comic strip I was reading slip out of my hands onto the table. One of my favorite pastimes was reading the Sunday comic strips. The sarcasm necessary to successfully pull off a witty comic strip is my jam. My mouth immediately felt like a desert, as if suddenly saliva is on short supply.

"My father?" I asked hesitantly, the word almost gets caught in my throat.

Then immediately ten thoughts invade my brain at once, demanding attention. *What does she mean, "see my father"? How does she know what my father looks like? Wait! Has she met my father? She knows him! When? Where? What the hell is happening? How long... how did... when did...* I couldn't finish any thought. They were all jumbled up. *My mother never said anything about my Aunt Barb knowing him. How would she?*

Wordlessly, Aunt Barb turned the picture around and slowly laid it on the table between us.

It was a 5 x 7 inch black and white photo and its age was revealed by the white border, so popular beginning in the '60s. Positioned landscaped, there were six people looking back at me. Three men on the right I didn't know, a man standing in the middle and then my Uncle Frank with his arm around my Aunt Barb's shoulders. Their outfits easily dated the fashion era of the '70s. The men wore some variety of tight-fitting, button-down disco shirts with giant winged collars. My Aunt Barb was in a short mini dress and white knee-high boots. They were all smiling at me, but the man in the middle was staring into what felt like my soul. It's his eyes. I knew those eyes. Those are my eyes.

"Those are...my eyes," I hear myself say, choking out the last two words.

Nobody has my eyes. Nobody has anything of mine. I felt the tears in my eyes, but they didn't fall. I can't describe it; I was so surprised but not sad. Maybe it's just relief that I was feeling. I do belong somewhere to someone. All the years of always standing out, never fitting in, and here he was with my eyes.

He stood what looked like a little over six feet judging by my uncle standing next to him. Maybe that's where I get my height. I'm 5'9". No woman in my family is taller than 5'6". Since sixth grade, I have spent my whole life towering over everyone. Always in the back row, too tall for front row status.

"The picture," my aunt said "was taken shortly after one of the band's gigs. Your Uncle Frank and I had gone to see them perform that night."

I had so many questions, like where was my mom? Did she take the picture? Was she even there? Did my Aunt Barb know about the two of them? So many questions, but not one of them passed my lips.

"Thank you," is all I said in the end, as I placed the picture in my purse.

———

I haven't thought much about that photo since then. Not until that seventh day before the naming ceremony, that is. Which may sound odd given all my emotions of feeling on the outside all the time. But here's the truth: I had a dad. His name was Arthur Roland Navarro, and he was one of the best human beings I ever had the pleasure of knowing. From third grade on, I never felt the absence of a father. I checked that box. He checked that box. That man loved me with all of his heart and was the best example of what a father should be. My gratitude has not wavered in this. So, I never gazed at that picture wishing for something that was missing, some vacancy never realized. I had a father.

But on the day of the ceremony, I had laid the baby on the bed. He was dressed in his fancy, ready-to-be-named outfit, and he looked so handsome. I grabbed my camera off the dresser to capture the moment when Jerry laid that picture next to our son. I did cry then. Hard giant tears. It felt like something inside of my womb, the place where he had lived just seven days ago, shifted. My heart expanded like there was no limit to its capacity. Lying on the bed was my heart outside of my body, all eight pounds of him, with my eyes. Had I not noticed before? Was I just so exhausted after the birth, trying to heal and figure out how to breastfeed while functioning off of no sleep?

He has my eyes. The baby has
his grandfather's eyes.

Slowly, I reached down for the picture and lowered the forgotten camera in my other hand. The baby, my baby, is identical to the man photographed twenty-four years ago in a small dive bar smiling, holding drum sticks in his hand and a secret in his heart.

All things feel full circle. Jerry is driving us home from the ceremony. I am sitting in the back seat staring down at a peacefully sleeping Kamau. I whisper his name over and over again to him, letting my love infuse each syllable. I never knew it was possible to love someone as much as I loved my son. I instantly knew there wouldn't be anything that I wouldn't do to keep him safe.

Maybe that's all my family was doing for me all those years. Maybe keeping my mother's affair and my Black heritage a secret was just their way of keeping me safe. Maybe they believed that truth would not have served me. *Maybe they believed their love would protect me from the rest of the world and all its painfully screwed up racist ways.* I didn't have those answers.

What I did know was that I was loved.

I knew my mother had felt the same way looking down at me twenty-three years ago in the folds of her dress in that two-door car bucket seat.

That she had made a similar vow then, to do everything she could to keep me safe.

We all chose our paths differently; my vow tonight is that will I love my son with all the truth I can muster.

CHAPTER 25

It was an evening wedding. The three of us wore all white. Traditional African dashiki and slacks for Jerry, a floor-length gown for me, loosely fitted, as I was nursing every couple of hours. For Kamau, a baby dashiki and pants that I spent ten minutes tugging over his bulky cloth diaper. At six months old, he was the definition of fat and happy. The Michelin tire man didn't have as many rolls as Kamau. Weighing in at a whopping twenty-four pounds, his rolls had rolls. Yes, he was ginormous with a permanent smile fixed to his lips. He laughed freely and often and his nearly black eyes twinkled with joy. I would sit for hours mesmerized by him. His joy nearly transfixed me. Kamau was so doggone happy to be born. Gleefully, Kamau baby babbled nearly every hour he was awake, yes even while nursing. His name meant quiet warrior and yet I can assure you, this child was never again quiet after his first day of life. Kamau was my heart outside of my body.

His dimples, just like his dad's, never quit. The joke for years was I married Jerry for his dimples. They ran deep in his family; everyone had a pair and I was obsessed with them. As a little girl, I'd spend hours in the bathroom mirror with my fingertips pressed into my cheeks, convinced I could make my own dimples. Truth be told, along with all his other wonderful qualities, I *was* marrying this man for his dimples.

Once again, our community of Black-conscious families congregated for our celebration. My closest girlfriends gathered in the master bedroom belonging to Bridgette and her husband, close friends of ours. Ma'at, Nicole, Bridgette, Tallibah, and Moyofune. We all were taking turns holding each other's babies during the preparation. In the past six months, each of us had birthed our first babies, except for Ma'at, midwife to us all; she had just had her fourth baby.

Nicole and I had formed a mommy's group, named Iya Ashe' (Mothers of Life), for holistically-minded women of color. Each month, we'd meet to support one another and of course share delicious meals together. Thirty of us first-time moms gathered and became each other's lifeline for this new role of motherhood we were journeying along. Now they were all here to support Jerry and I exchanging our vows.

What Jerry and I had not shared with anyone except our guides (think best man and matron of honor), was that our wedding would have a naming ceremony aspect to it as well. We had been talking about it for months now. We had met in the pursuit of learning our African ancestral heritage; now we wanted to fully live an African- centered lifestyle. Yet here we were lugging around names that no longer reflected who we were. The decision had been an easy one for us. It made the most sense and felt right to change our names. We also knew so many that had already embarked on that journey. Only six months ago, we had been given a family last name, now it was time to decide the fate of our first names. It was decided. I was to choose his first name and he was to choose mine and the names would be revealed and blessed at our wedding.

Like Kamau's naming ceremony, our wedding embodied African traditions from many regions. Symbolizing all the aspects of life, there was honey for the easy times, lemon for the sour, oil for the times needed to soothe over things and to forgive, water to cleanse away bitter times and ill feelings, and coconut for the times to celebrate. A beautiful white clothed path was created that we were to walk along together; some parts had rose petals symbolizing the easy times, other parts had small sticks and roughage for the challenges that awaited us. We washed one another's feet and then our guides blindfolded us, symbolizing the foundation of faith that marriage required through all times. Our promise to each other was to always be there for one another, so fingers intertwined together we began the blindfolded journey along the clothed path. Each of our guides stood on the side, gently offering support but not interfering.

At the end of the pathway, our blindfolds removed, we shared our vows then our names. Though I had searched and searched, not one word encompassed everything I believed the man I loved to be. So, me being me, I changed the rules and gave him two names.

Sekou—wise and educated.

Yakini—honest and truth teller.

I held my breath when Sekou began sharing why he had made his choice. Nervous, yet excited that he would have found a name he believed symbolized who I was. A name that saw me. A name not based on a lie. Barbara never belonged to me. It was always borrowed. I had spent twenty-three years carrying an ill-fitting name. I had been named after my grandmother, whom I loved dearly, yet the irony was that name had always been foreign to me. Like someone who becomes fluent in a second language, but their accent is so distinct it's difficult to understand them.

Sekou continues, "The name transcends languages, cultures, and regions encompassing many meanings, each more beautiful than the next. Your name: Kindhearted. Benevolent. Blissful. Blessed. In Arabic it means Eden or place of return, in the Qur'an the prophecy speaks of it as everlasting comfort of mankind."

My face flushes and my heart is so full with love, he sees me. Sekou's favorite jazz musician of all times is John Coltrane, an African American saxophonist. My love for jazz today comes from Sekou's deep appreciation of the genre. John Coltrane wrote a beautiful ballad to his wife, and he named the song after her. When I was pregnant, we'd spend hours listening to jazz artists of Sekou's choosing. I'd lay in between our giant floor speakers bathing my pregnant belly in the melodies. Unbeknownst to me, John Coltrane had been playing his ballad for our son. On countless evenings that song had lulled me to sleep.

Sekou slowly says the name, pronouncing each syllable. *"Nye-ee-mah."*

The word washes over me like a powerful wave of comprehension.

And suddenly I understand.

This moment was always coming.

This woman, this version of me, had always been here, waiting for me to arrive. Waiting for me to experience all that I had, the struggles, the trials, the loves, the pain, and the joys. She'd been there beckoning me forward, encouraging me, crying with me, cheering me, loving me.

I looked up into Sekou's eyes. He did it. Tears streaming down my cheeks.

He did it. Truth has a resonance. A vibration that stirs your soul.

I finally exhale.

Naeema had always been here waiting for me.

EPILOGUE

WHAT I KNOW FOR SURE...

Vulnerability is necessary.

Faith is essential.

Human connection is vital.

What keeps us from connection is believing we are not worthy of connection.

Worthiness comes from a strong sense of love and belonging.

People who have that strong sense, believe they are worth having love and belonging.

I was raised with love yet had no sense of belonging.

WHAT I LEARNED...

I am not my experiences.

I am a whole being that has had some unfortunate encounters.

I am also a woman who has been blessed by people and her adventures.

Shame lives in the dark.

Animated by secrecy, silence, and judgement.

I spent a lifetime covering mine up.

Turns out vulnerability was my light all along.

These pages, woven from pain turned courage, are my light manifested.

WHO I'VE BECOME...

I am brave.

I am who I am because of the trials I have endured.

I am a better human being because of the people who have carved a place in my life.

I have had deep meaningful relationships.

I have loved fully and hard.

I have experienced joy on a level I never thought possible.

I have withstood loss and trauma that damn near buried me.

Healing is a journey, so buckle up.

Prayer, therapy, tribe support and self-love gave me perspective, empathy and a heart to serve.

I practiced compassion for myself and learned to give grace to others.

I am grateful for all my experiences, even the awful ones.

I do not sit in victimhood nor do I wish those things had never happened.

Most days, I see them for the blessings they are and I bless those who contributed to my healing.

My experiences have given me the capacity to love more, give more, become more, and do more, all from a place of abundance.

And...

I. Am. A. Work. In. Progress.

WHAT I HOPE FOR YOU...

Be Outrageously Vulnerable

SUGGESTED READING LIST

Alexander, Michelle. *The New Jim Crow: Mass Incarceration in the Age of Colorblindness.*

Ani, Marimba. *Yurugu: An African-Centered Critique of European Cultural Thought and Behavior.*

Blackmon, Douglas A. *Slavery by Another Name: The Re-Enslavement of Black Americans from the Civil War to World War II.*

Bradley, Michael. *The Iceman Inheritance: Prehistoric Sources of Western Man's Racism, Sexism and Aggression.*

DiAngelo, Robin. *White Fragility: Why It's So Hard for White People to Talk About Racism.*

Du Bois, W.E.B. *The Souls of Black Folk.*

Haley, Alex. *The Autobiography of Malcolm X.*

Lynch, Willie. *The Willie Lynch Letter and the Making of a Slave.*

Rothstein, Richard. *The Color of Law: A Forgotten History of How Our Government Segregated America.*

Van Sertima, Ivan. *The Lost Sciences of Africa: An Overview.*

Van Sertima, Ivan. *They Came Before Columbus: The African Presence in Ancient America.*

Welsing, Dr. Frances Cress. *The Isis Papers: The Keys to the Colors.*

Williams, Chancellor. *Destruction of Black Civilization: Great Issues of a Race from 4500 BC to 2000 AD.*

Woodson, Carter G. *The Mis-Education of the Negro.*

ACKNOWLEDGMENTS

Words cannot encompass the gratitude that flows through me for the Universal presence I call God.

Thanking everyone can be a risky feat. Please know that you, yes you, hold a special place in my heart's memory for extending love, grace, wisdom, patience, and joy to me.

Kamau and Kinan for their unending love and allowing me to stay in my room for hours at a time, mostly undisturbed.

William, my baby brother, the only regret I have is wishing I had been the older sister you deserved.

My entrepreneur road dogs, Monica and Sonza, for literally coming to pick me up off the floor, then holding a twenty-four-hour vigil for weeks until I could stand on my own. I've never felt that broken and supported at the same time. For loving me while I cried in my soup to "sage-ing" my practice and adorning me with healing crystals.

Stephanie and Modupe for holding it down at EFC and supporting me no matter how crazy I became.

All of my EFC Practice Members for all the book therapy during your adjustments.

Ernest for literally spending every single Friday afternoon with me as the best damn therapist for over six months and counting. Thank you for guiding me along the journey to pull back the rug and heal my ignored trauma.

Nicole (the sister I always dreamed of) for everything and also answering the phone and talking me down from the ledge each time I wanted to "skip the whole damn thing."

Uncle Frank for being my historian.

Tina and Yolanda for reminding me that I had everything I needed to succeed.

My Mom2Mom crew for cheerleading like no others.

Yvonne for being the best volunteer marketing expert.

Kat I loved you the moment I sat on your lap first quarter and because professional campaign advising is just in you.

Laura Schlom for everything we share and being my very first supporter.

Daimeyon Williams...damn baby.

Special thank you to three amazing women who paused their own lives to put an *extra sweet layer of goodness* on this book:

Elise Wilder

Stacey Sanders

Kathy Mansfield

Professor Eric Koester for saying yes to your calling and creating a magical program for us would-be authors.

The whole New Degree Press team, especially Mike Butler and Kaity Van Riper for their angelic editing blessings that I'll never be able to repay.

Amanda for being my secret superpower and enduring all my messiness for two years and upgrading my game at every turn!

Thank you all for believing in this book before it ever was a book!

Anita Daniels

Mysti French

Danny Lamonte

Kellie Jackson

Jeremy Coleman

Dr. Tarryn Foster

Lori-Ann Harper

Chi Johnson

Tru Johnson

Brittany Waites

Andrea Harvel

Sagine Saphire Belizaire

Lydell J. Gunsby

Jennifer M. Gust

Carol Smith Sparkman

Christopher T. Roach

Stewart Joslin

Chris A. Carrier

Synovia Jones

Kanani Briggs

Kristina Maybin

Leilani Raglin

Jabar Ali

Jay Hurt

Alexander Harris

Melissa Pappion

Mynor Rivera

Sharon Hines Bent

India Campbell

Ernestine Nesby

Lusekelo Mbisa

Shaniqua Wright

Kina Lane

Gwendolyn Ferrell

James Roberts II

Sheree Thompson

Makeda Minott

Steven Robinson

Valerie Murray

Tonja Flores

Kailei Carr

Eric Koester

LaShawna Hughes

Miguel McNair

Jermaine Robb

Dwayne Miller

Jennifer Thomas

Lonnie Robinson

Marita Thompson

Kristin Morris

Kevin W. Mahdi

Kendrick McQueen

Akeaba Williams
Craig Johnson
Kim Bessinger
Denise Harris
Erin Fletcher
Bilby and Nhi Anthonio
Elaine Harris
Kathryn Shirley
Milt Jordan
Jojuyounghi Cleaver
Kelly Klippel
Desiree Smith
Kina Lane
Susan Johnson
Lorri Dorce-Clark
Dale Cartwright
Richard Horton
Mark Wallace
Veronica P. Wall
Dr. Sonza Curtis
Nadina Weatherson
Pasqueal Bigoms
Anthony R. Lloyd
Jaffany Finch
Melsean A. Shaw
Rashunda Lafaye
Crystal Hickman
Shannelle Santiago
Shaun Phifer
Kevin Smith
Nicole Pacheco
LaBelle Bryan

Monica Beckham
Valerie Hunter
Nick Nelson
Susan Johnson
Morgan Wider
Konstance A. McCullah
Tara Lokan
Tom Georges
Leah Merriweather
Tricia Johnson

APPENDIX

CHAPTER 3

Blad, Evie. "Bill Addresses Cultural Genocide Caused by Indian Boarding Schools." Education Week. October 01, 2020. Accessed June 4, 2021. *https://www. edweek.org/policy-politics/bill-addresses-cultural-geno-cide-caused-by-indian-boarding-schools/2020/10?s_kwcid =AL!6416!3!486544088589!b!!g!!&utm_source=goog&utm_ medium=cpc&utm_campaign=ew+dynamic+recent%20 &ccid=dynamic+ads+recent+articles&ccag=recent+articles+- dynamic&cckw=&cccv=dynamic+ad&gclid=CjoKCQjw5JSL- BhCxARIsAHgO2Sd4VrAGVS2LDacJ4np-Y6Sq9kcdJoxaS- jYrlabjZom1jU4XTuYzZRsaAm5UEALw_wcB*

"Broken Promises: Continuing Federal Funding Shortfall for Native Americans." Briefing before the United States Commission on Civil Rights. Washington, DC: Briefing Report December 2018. *https://www.usccr.gov/files/pubs/2018/12-20- Broken-Promises.pdf.*

Maxwell, Lesli A. "Thousands of Indigenous Students Died in Boarding Schools." Education Week. January 07, 2014. *https://*

www.edweek.org/leadership/thousands-of-indigenous-students-died-in-canadian-boarding-schools-panel-finds/2014/01.

"The Meriam Report: The Problem of Indian Administration." National Indian Law Library. 1928. Accessed on June 25, 2021. *https://narf.org/nill/resources/meriam.html.*

Van Cott, John W. "Online Utah." Accessed June 4, 2021. *https://onlineutah.us/randletthistory.shtml.*

CHAPTER 11

"Malcolm." July 4, 2021. *https://malcolmx.com/biography.*

X, Malcolm. *The Autobiography of Malcolm X.* New York: Bantam Doubleday Dell Publishing Group, 1998.

CHAPTER 12

Southern California Tribal Chairmen's Association. "Chemeheuvi Indian Tribe." 2021. *https://sctca.net/chemehuevi-indian-tribe.*

CHAPTER 13

Alexander, Michelle. *The New Jim Crow: Mass Incarceration in the Age of Colorblindness.* New York: The New Press, 2020.

Feder-Haugabook, Ayala. "Latasha Harlins (1975–1991)." Black Past. September 14, 2017. Accessed on August 5, 2021. *https://www.blackpast.org/african-american-history/harlins-latasha-1975-1991.*

CHAPTER 14

Blatch, Sydella. "Great Achievements in Science and Technology in Ancient Africa." *ASBMB Today*. February 1, 2013. *https://www.asbmb.org/asbmb-today/science/020113/great-achievements-in-stem-in-ancient-africa*.

"1921 Tulsa Race Massacre." Tulsa Historical Society and Museum. Museum and Society. 2021. Accessed June 1, 2021. *https://www.tulsahistory.org/exhibit/1921-tulsa-race-massacre/*

Van Sertima, I. "The Lost Sciences of Africa: An Overview." *Blacks in Science: Ancient and Modern*. New Jersey: Transaction Publishers, 1983.

Woods, Geraldine. *Science in Ancient Egypt*. New York: Franklin Watts, 1988.

Zaslavsky, C. "The Yoruba Number System." *Blacks in Science: Ancient and Modern*. New Jersey: Transaction Publishers, 1983.

CHAPTER 18

Adams, H. "African Observers of the Universe: The Sirius Question." *Blacks in Science: Ancient and Modern*. New Jersey: Transaction Publishers, 1983.

Asante, M. *et al.* "Great Zimbabwe: An Ancient African City-State." *Blacks in Science: Ancient and Modern*. New Jersey: Transaction Publishers, 1983.

Bennett, Alice. "Ancient African Civilizations." The Collector. Accessed on June 20, 2021. *https://www.thecollector.com/ ancient-african-civilizations.*

Brooks, L. *African Achievements: Leaders, Civilizations and Cultures of Ancient Africa.* New York: De Gustibus Press, 1971.

Lynch, B. M. and L.H. Robbins, "Namoratunga: The First Archeoastronomical Evidence in Sub-Saharan Afraica." *Science.* 1978. Accessed June 13, 2021. *https://www.science.org/ doi/10.1126/science.200.4343.766.*

MacDonald, K.C., Roderick Grierson and Jamila White. *Explore the Wonders.* PBS. Accessed on July 28, 2021. *https://www.pbs. org/wonders/fr_wn.htm*

Van Sertima, I. *They Came Before Columbus: The African Presence in Ancient America.* New York: Random House. 1976.

CHAPTER 19

Alexander, Michelle. *The New Jim Crow: Mass Incarceration in the Age of Colorblindness.* New York: The New Press, 2020.

Hassett-Walker, Connie. "How You Start is How You Finish? The Slave Patrol and Jim Crow Origins of Policing." American Bar Association. January 11, 2021. Accessed on August 1, 2021. *https://www.americanbar.org/groups/crsj/publications/ human_rights_magazine_home/civil-rights-reimagining-policing/how-you-start-is-how-you-finish/*